P9-DUZ-818

QUICK
GREEN JOBS GUIDE

Six Steps to a Green Career

Laurence Shatkin, Ph.D.

Contents

JIST Works
America's Career Publisher®

Quick Green Jobs Guide

© 2011 by JIST Publishing

Published by JIST Works, an imprint of JIST Publishing
7321 Shadeland Station, Suite 200
Indianapolis, Indiana 46256-3923
Phone: 800-648-JIST   Fax: 877-454-7839   E-mail: info@jist.com   Web site: www.jist.com

---

Some Other Books by Laurence Shatkin, PhD

2011 Career Plan	40 Best Fields for Your Career
Best Jobs for the 21st Century	225 Best Jobs for Baby Boomers
200 Best Jobs for College Graduates	250 Best-Paying Jobs
300 Best Jobs Without a Four-Year Degree	150 Best Jobs for a Better World
200 Best Jobs Through Apprenticeships	200 Best Jobs for Introverts
50 Best Jobs for Your Personality	150 Best Recession-Proof Jobs

---

Quantity discounts are available for JIST products. Please call 800-648-JIST or visit www.jist.com for a free catalog and more information.

Visit www.jist.com for information on JIST, tables of contents, sample pages, and ordering information on our many products.

Acquisitions Editor: Susan Pines
Development Editor: Stephanie Koutek
Cover and Interior Designer: Aleata Halbig
Interior Layout: Aleata Halbig
Proofreader: Jeanne Clark

Printed in the United States of America

15 14 13 12 11 10   9 8 7 6 5 4 3 2 1

We have been careful to provide accurate information throughout this book, but it is possible that errors and omissions have been introduced. Please consider this in making any career plans or other important decisions. Trust your own judgment above all else and in all things.

Package of 10
ISBN 978-1-59357-849-7

STEP 1: Identify Three Types of Green Jobs

To understand the term *green job*, you first need to understand what a *sustainable* economy is. Our planet's population is close to 7 billion and is expected to reach about 9 billion by 2050. At the rate that we're now using up our planet's supply of fossil fuels and raw materials, we won't have enough of these vital resources to support Earth's population. That's why we are shifting away from using up resources and toward using resources that are renewable in ways that are not wasteful. That's an economy that we can sustain, a green economy.

What resources are renewable? Sunshine, wind, and the heat of Earth's interior can never get used up and can produce electric power. Growing plants can be sown and harvested year after year and can be turned into fuel.

One of the basic principles of economics is that *everything has a cost.* Some things used to be so plentiful that we considered them free. Take clean air, for example. In the olden days, when Earth's population was small and not much fuel was being burned, nobody thought about the cost of putting smoke into the air. Nowadays, however, the costs are being felt in many ways: in cases of asthma, which is the fastest-growing chronic disease; in the fisheries that have been destroyed by acid rain; and, worst of all, in the many hardships we will endure as heat-trapping gases warm up our planet.

Once you realize that clean air has a cost, you realize we all pay the costs when businesses spew smoke from their chimneys and drivers emit fumes from their tailpipes. That's not fair!

In a green economy, everyone pays the true costs of what they're doing. You may already have noticed small signs of this trend. Perhaps your local supermarket charges a few cents for throw-away grocery bags or gives a few cents' discount to people who don't use them. You may have heard about businesses that buy a "carbon offset": To compensate for carbon dioxide that they're emitting, they pay for trees to be planted somewhere to soak up an equivalent amount of the greenhouse gas.

Many businesses and individuals will not willingly pay these costs, so governments levy taxes and fines to prevent costly behavior: air pollution, water pollution, littering, trash dumping, and overfishing. Congress has considered a carbon tax or a "cap-and-trade" law so that emitting carbon dioxide becomes part of the cost of doing business.

Once businesses start paying all the true costs of their activities, another principle of economics applies: *When one way of doing business becomes too costly, successful businesses find another way.* Business leaders, with the help of scientists and engineers, are discovering ways to recycle wastes and conserve energy.

It costs money to hire workers and update processes to make these changes, but business leaders are discovering that, even in the short run, investments in conservation and green technologies can save them money. For example, Walmart (which is famous for elevating cost-cutting above all other business considerations) has been improving the fuel efficiency of its fleet of trucks after realizing that each extra mile per gallon will save more than $52 million per year. All new Walmart stores are being built with skylights that allow indoor lights to be dimmed during the day, and in California the new stores have heat-reflecting white roofs.

Probably the biggest push toward a green economy is the problem of global warming. The occasional bad snowstorm doesn't change the fact that Earth as a whole is warming up. Scientists are overwhelmingly convinced that the chief cause is carbon dioxide that we're pumping into the atmosphere each time we burn oil, coal, or other fuels. If we continue on our present path, we will see crop failures, dried-up water sources, more violent storms, extinction of wildlife, and coastal flooding just a few decades from now. Whatever we can do to use less energy or switch to renewable energy sources will slow down or even reverse global warming.

Despite what you may have heard, changing to a green economy does not have to harm our standard of living. Californians are living as comfortably as people in most other states, yet their state has held its per-capita energy use at the same level since 1974, while nationwide that rate has increased by 50 percent.

On balance, the green economy will create many job opportunities. These green jobs are the focus of this book.

The Three Kinds of Green Jobs

Every big shift in the economy creates many new job opportunities. Think about what happened when computers arrived. They created many new occupations, such as computer programmers and computer systems analysts. But more important was the way technology changed existing occupations. By 2001, 56 percent of all workers were using computers, but only a small fraction of these workers had the word "computer" in their job title.

Something very similar is expected to happen to careers as we shift to a green economy. The U.S. Department of Labor identifies three kinds of occupations that will contribute to the green economy. About one-third of the jobs included in this book belong to each of these three types:

- **Green Increased-Demand Occupations:** These existing jobs will take on many new workers as green practices and technologies expand. The work itself and the skill requirements will not change much.

- **Green Enhanced-Skills Occupations:** These existing jobs will experience changes in work tasks and skill requirements as we shift to a green economy. They may or may not see increases in employment.

- **Green New and Emerging Occupations:** These jobs are being created to do new kinds of work or meet new skill requirements.

These definitions point to an important truth: **Most green work opportunities will be in *existing* occupations.** That's why this book can exist even though the green economy has not fully emerged yet.

How to Make Your Job Greener

No matter what job you hold, you can make it greener. Once you understand how the business works, you probably can think of ways to conserve energy, recycle, or economize on raw materials. Your employer will welcome money-saving ideas for green practices, such as turning off computers at night, controlling bathroom lights with a motion detector, or making two-sided copies. If your idea requires an investment of some kind, such as purchasing more energy-efficient equipment, you can help make your case by calculating how soon the investment will pay for itself in savings.

Even if you're working in an occupation that's not included in this book, you might be able to "work green" by finding a job in a green industry. For example, accountants, business analysts, and meeting planners are needed just as much by clean-energy-producing companies or recycling companies as by other kinds of businesses.

You also can pursue green interests in your time off work. Find (or start) a volunteer group that works to improve the environment of your community or is active in green political causes. Look for ways to make your lifestyle greener by cutting energy use in your home, reducing the amount of energy used to produce your food, recycling materials, and burning less gasoline on the highways.

Key Points: Step 1

- In a green (sustainable) economy, resources are renewable and are used in ways that are not wasteful.

- Green practices save money for businesses and create job opportunities.

- Most green work opportunities will be in existing occupations.

STEP 2: Learn About Green Industries

Now that you understand what a green job is, it's time to look at some of the different things green workers do. These workers aren't all installing solar panels or servicing wind turbines. In fact, the U.S. Department of Labor has identified 12 industry sectors where these workers contribute to a green economy. Let's look at each sector—what it does and what job titles are found in it. As you read about the green industries, think about which kinds of work you want to be involved in.

Renewable Energy Generation

This industry sector covers activities related to developing and using renewable energy sources such as solar, wind, geothermal, and biomass.

You're probably familiar with the solar panels that convert sunlight directly into electricity—these are called *photovoltaic (PV) systems.* You may be less familiar with *solar thermal systems,* which soak up the heat from sunlight to provide hot water that warms a house or swimming pool or serves an industrial use.

America is well endowed with *wind energy,* especially on the Great Plains and along our coasts, and recent years have seen the development of many new wind farms of huge turbines that generate electricity.

Geothermal energy projects tap into the heat of rock formations beneath Earth's surface. Hot water pumped from these sources can be used to heat buildings and for industrial processes such as drying. It can also be used to power steam turbines and similar devices to generate electricity.

Hydroelectric power is America's second-most-widely used renewable energy source, generating electricity from turbines installed next to dams or at places such as Niagara Falls where water naturally falls from a height. Some other forms of hydropower are presently in highly limited use or are still experimental; these derive power from tides or waves or from the current within a stream (similar to a wind turbine turning in the breeze).

Long ago, plants perfected a process for capturing and storing solar energy as sugars, starches, oils, and woody tissue. Unlike deposits of coal and oil, plants can be grown year after year, and as they grow they absorb carbon dioxide from the air. The most time-honored way to extract energy from plants is to burn the *biomass* as fuel. A more versatile process is to heat the biomass with limited oxygen and thus produce a synthetic gas fuel ("syngas"), a mixture of carbon monoxide and hydrogen. Power generation from biomass is particularly appealing because it provides a use for crop residues, timber trimmings, paper waste, and other plant byproducts.

Other plant products can be chemically processed into *biofuels,* such as corn-derived ethanol and diesel fuel made from discarded cooking oil. Scientists and engineers are actively working on new ways to produce alcohol and diesel-ready oils from plant sources that are more energy-efficient than corn or soybeans, such as switchgrass and algae.

The Renewable Energy Generation industry sector also includes traditional, nonrenewable sources of energy undergoing significant green technological changes. For example, some coal-fired power plants are mixing coal with powdered, charred biomass. Others are using the integrated gasification combined cycle (IGCC) technique, which heats coal to produce syngas and removes impurities from the gas before burning it. Nuclear power is becoming more popular because its byproducts, although hard to handle, are a local problem rather than a global problem.

Generating energy requires technicians, managers, site locators, and many other workers. Some of these workers will come from old energy industries—for example, oil drilling—and apply their skills to new forms of energy production. Here are the occupations included in this book that work in this industry sector:

> Biofuels Production Workers
>
> Biomass Energy Production Workers
>
> Electrical and Electronics Repairers, Powerhouse, Substation, and Relay
>
> Engineering and Natural Sciences Managers
>
> Engineers
>
> Geothermal Energy Production Workers
>
> Glaziers
>
> Hydroelectric Energy Production Workers
>
> Power Plant Operators, Distributors, and Dispatchers
>
> Science Technicians
>
> Sheet Metal Workers
>
> Solar Energy Production Workers
>
> Wind Energy Production Workers

Transportation

This industry sector covers activities related to increasing efficiency or reducing the environmental impact of various forms of transportation, including trucking, mass transit, and freight rail.

Our economy depends on moving goods and people from place to place, but these activities consume a lot of energy: two-thirds of our oil consumption and 28 percent of our total energy use. As we shift to a green economy, we are finding more efficient techniques. For example, manufacturers are outsourcing their distribution functions to trucking and warehousing companies that can perform these tasks with greater efficiency. Increased use of freight rail is another way to save energy; one estimate is that a truck consumes 70 percent more fuel to haul the same load.

To get commuters out of their cars and into trains and buses, state and local governments have been subsidizing and expanding mass transit lines. Some cities have created bicycle lanes on major streets.

Transportation requires vehicle drivers, route planners, dispatchers, managers, and many other workers. Here are some of the green occupations in this industry sector:

> Engineering Technicians
> Engineers

Energy Efficiency

This industry sector covers activities related to increasing energy efficiency, constructing "smart grids," and other energy-efficient activities.

America's electric power industry is moving toward creation of a smart grid that routes power efficiently, accommodates the shifting power outputs of resources such as sunshine and wind, and responds quickly to disruptions. A smart grid might communicate with your washing machine so that you could set the appliance to do a load of laundry at whatever time of night power is most available; the utility company could charge you a cheaper rate for this off-peak use.

Some efficient practices consist of using energy from unlikely places. For example, in most parts of the United States, the groundwater or the soil just a few feet below the surface maintains a constant temperature throughout the year. Heat pumps, which work like air conditioners in reverse, can concentrate the heat below the surface and use it to warm a building in winter. In summer, the same process can be reversed to air condition the building with greater efficiency than traditional air-cooled equipment can achieve.

In industry, engineers are finding ways to match up processes that produce waste heat with processes that consume heat.

Power distributors, engineers, technicians, and many other workers are engaged in increasing energy efficiency. Here are some of the green occupations in this industry sector:

Boilermakers

Computer Systems Analysts

Energy Auditors

Engineers

Fuel Cell Technicians

Heating, Air-Conditioning, and Refrigeration Mechanics and Installers

Industrial Ecologists

Insulation Workers

Line Installers and Repairers

Weatherization Installers and Technicians

Green Construction

This industry sector covers activities related to constructing new green buildings, retrofitting residential and commercial buildings, and using green practices in any construction activities.

Construction in the United States has long been guided by building codes that ensure safety (for example, electrical wiring that won't start fires). Some new codes are being developed to aid the shift to a green economy. The best-known of these are the LEED (Leadership in Energy and Environmental Design) standards, which are designed to ensure that a building meets green requirements for sustainable site development, water savings, energy efficiency, materials selection, and indoor environmental quality. Another set of standards, the International Green Construction Code (IGCC), is still under development as of this writing.

The green practice of recycling can be applied to whole buildings: Architects and real estate developers are finding ways to update old buildings for new uses as residential, commercial, or industrial spaces. Imaginative designers can sometimes find dramatic new uses for old real estate. For example, New York City recently transformed an old elevated railway line into an elevated city park. Even if the owners of a building do not want to change its function, they may want to make it more energy-efficient by adding insulation, skylights, solar panels, or an improved heating and cooling system.

Construction companies are learning how to apply green practices to many aspects of their projects. They may choose architectural features that conserve energy, such as rooftop shrubbery or walls that absorb solar heat. Sustainable building materials such as straw bales and bamboo or recycled materials such as old barn timbers and used bricks are replacing newly cut wood in some projects.

To meet the needs of green construction, architects, construction managers, carpenters, roofers, and many other tradesworkers will learn and apply new skills. Here are some of the green occupations in this industry sector:

Architects, Except Landscape and Naval

Boilermakers

Brownfield Redevelopment Specialists and Site Managers

Carpenters

Construction and Building Inspectors

Construction Laborers

Construction Managers

Drafters

Electricians

Engineers

First-Line Supervisors/Managers of Construction Trades and Extraction Workers

Glaziers

Hazardous Materials Removal Workers

Heating, Air-Conditioning, and Refrigeration Mechanics and Installers

Insulation Workers

Landscape Architects

Plumbers, Pipelayers, Pipefitters, and Steamfitters

Roofers

Sheet Metal Workers

Surveyors, Cartographers, Photogrammetrists, and Surveying and Mapping Technicians

Urban and Regional Planners

Welding, Soldering, and Brazing Workers

Energy Trading

This industry sector covers financial services related to buying and selling energy as an economic commodity, as well as carbon trading projects.

Energy trading employs many financial experts, but none of the green jobs described in this book is associated with this industry sector.

Energy and Carbon Capture and Storage

This industry sector covers activities related to capturing and storing energy or carbon emissions.

Compared to other sources of energy, coal is so cheap and plentiful in the United States that power-generating companies are looking for ways to capture and store the carbon dioxide gas that burning coal produces. One approach is to liquefy the gas and inject the fluid deep underground ("carbon sequestration"). Some engineers are working on a process that mimics sea creatures by combining the gas with minerals from seawater to create a cement that's much like coral or seashells.

Everyone is familiar with using batteries to store energy, but present battery technology is not an economical way to store utility-level quantities of electricity in most regions of the United States. Hydropower is proving more useful: Water can be pumped uphill from a lower reservoir to a higher one, and then later released to flow downhill through a turbine. Although this cycle consumes more energy than it produces, it can be useful to even out temporary mismatches between power that is available and power that is needed by customers. Similarly, more than 1,000 buildings in California are now getting air-conditioning equipment that freezes 450-gallon blocks of ice overnight, when power costs are low, and uses the ice to cool indoor air during the day. Because wind and sunshine vary in availability, the more those power sources are used, the more pumped-storage hydropower, ice-based air conditioning, and other energy-storage technologies will be needed.

Engineers, technicians, power plant operators, and many other workers are engaged in capturing and storing energy and carbon. The one occupation described in this book that belongs in this industry sector is Power Plant Operators, Distributors, and Dispatchers.

Research, Design, and Consulting Services

This industry sector covers activities such as energy consulting or research and other related business services.

In this step, you're reading about many practices and technologies that businesses are adopting to be more green. In most cases, business owners and managers did not invent or implement these ideas on their own. Researchers discovered the principles that make these ideas work. Engineers designed and perfected the technologies that turned the ideas into useful products and practices. Consultants worked with the businesses to roll out these new ways of doing business, to train workers in applying them, and in some cases to convince investors and the public to accept them.

Scientists, engineers, technicians, trainers, and many other workers are needed to provide research, design, and consulting services. Here are some of the green occupations in this industry sector:

Architects, Except Landscape and Naval

Chemists and Materials Scientists

Computer Systems Analysts

Engineering and Natural Sciences Managers

Engineering Technicians

Engineers

Geoscientists and Hydrologists

Landscape Architects

Physicists and Astronomers

Science Technicians

Urban and Regional Planners

Environmental Protection

This industry sector covers activities related to environmental remediation, climate change adaptation, and ensuring or enhancing air quality.

As we transition to a green economy, a lot of previous environmental damage needs to be fixed, and more will occur. The 2010 BP oil spill in the Gulf of Mexico—an estimated 206 million gallons—was one of the more spectacular environmental disasters of recent years, but much damage occurs more gradually and without a single, obvious source. For example, it's estimated that amateur mechanics and other Americans annually dump more than 240 million gallons of oil improperly.

Many abandoned industrial sites are polluted with asbestos, solvents, PCBs, or other toxic chemicals. These can become excellent locations for new businesses once they have undergone extensive cleanup, so specialized engineers and managers are directing projects to rehabilitate the sites. Other specialists are reclaiming land that has been scarred by mining, waterways that have been polluted, and wetlands that have been drained.

As Earth's climate warms up, many new problems are emerging. Rainfall patterns are changing, affecting agricultural practices and wildlife habitats. Pests may extend their geographic range or their yearly periods of infestation and get out of sync with predators that formerly controlled them. Researchers are working to identify which of these trends are temporary setbacks and which indicate permanent change. They are also advising farmers, timber lot managers, ski resort owners, and others in weather-dependent businesses on how to adapt to these changes.

Other workers are monitoring air quality, pinpointing air polluters, and helping businesses adopt practices and technologies that will control releases of waste gases and smoke particles.

Protecting the environment requires the work of planners, scientists, engineers, technicians, and many others. Here are some of the green occupations in this industry sector:

> Biological Scientists
>
> Conservation Scientists and Foresters
>
> Construction Managers
>
> Engineering and Natural Sciences Managers
>
> Engineering Technicians
>
> Engineers
>
> Environmental Restoration Planners
>
> Environmental Scientists and Specialists
>
> Forest and Conservation Workers
>
> Geoscientists and Hydrologists
>
> Hazardous Materials Removal Workers
>
> Landscape Architects
>
> Science Technicians
>
> Water and Liquid Waste Treatment Plant and System Operators
>
> Water Resource Specialists

Agriculture and Forestry

This industry sector covers activities related to using natural pesticides, efficient land management or farming, and aquaculture.

What could be greener than agriculture? Yet not all agricultural practices are sustainable. Excessive use of toxic pesticides, fertilizer runoff, manure buildup at factory farms, and clear-cutting of forests are some of the ways that agriculture and forestry can put stress on the environment. Sustainable alternatives to these practices are catching on. For example, a better understanding of the life cycle of pests often allows farmers to sharply reduce their use of pesticides or switch to natural substances with less broad-spectrum impact.

Agricultural scientists, farm managers, food technicians, and other workers are needed to make agriculture and forestry truly green. Here are some of the green occupations in this industry sector:

> Conservation Scientists and Foresters
>
> Farmers, Ranchers, and Agricultural Managers

Forest and Conservation Workers

Landscape Architects

Science Technicians

Manufacturing

This industry sector covers activities related to the manufacturing of green materials needed in other sectors of the economy, such as construction and energy generation. It also covers the shift to energy-efficient manufacturing processes.

The transition to a green economy will require many new manufactured goods, from high-efficiency LED lights to battery-powered automobiles. Many workers will be needed to operate the equipment that manufactures these products and to manage industrial processes in ways that reduce costs and keep factories open in America. To work with highly automated manufacturing processes, including robotics, workers in this industry sector will need to be more skilled than they were in the past.

For several years now, industry has embraced *lean manufacturing*, the practice of eliminating all waste in manufacturing processes—that is, all tasks and byproducts that do not add value for the customer. This practice is now expanding to recognize environmental waste, which includes inefficient use of raw materials, the costs of waste disposal, and the costs of pollution control. Greener production processes, including the use of more nature-friendly materials, can greatly reduce these costs.

Green manufacturing requires technicians, efficiency experts, production managers, and many other skilled workers. Here are some of the green occupations in this industry sector:

Engineering Technicians

Engineers

Glaziers

Industrial Machinery Mechanics and Millwrights

Science Technicians

Sheet Metal Workers

Welding, Soldering, and Brazing Workers

Recycling and Waste Reduction

This industry sector covers activities related to solid waste and wastewater management, treatment, and reduction, as well as processing recyclable materials.

Many communities in the United States are running out of places to dump their garbage, and they are recognizing that existing dumps and incinerators can release harmful substances into the soil, water, and air. To reduce the waste stream, many communities are encouraging recycling of waste materials that are easy to reprocess, such as paper, glass, metal, and some plastics.

Manufacturers are also discovering ways to reduce their waste production. The Subaru plant in Indiana and the Honda plant in Alabama turn out hundreds of thousands of cars per year without adding an ounce of waste to a landfill. They recycle steel from car parts, paper and plastic from packaging, solvents from paint, wood from pallets, and even leftover food from the cafeteria.

Garbage dumps produce waste of their own that can be recycled: a mixture of gases, about half of which is methane, which is called natural gas when it's found in oil wells. Methane in the atmosphere traps 23 times as much heat as carbon dioxide, so its release needs to be controlled, but fortunately it has commercial value. Waste management companies have developed ways to tap into landfills, extract the gas, filter it, purify it, compress it, and sell it. On some farms and feedlots, a similar gas byproduct is collected from decaying animal manure.

Technicians, engineers, production managers, and many other workers take part in recycling and waste reduction activities. Here are some of the occupations in this industry sector:

> Brownfield Redevelopment Specialists and Site Managers
>
> Hazardous Materials Removal Workers
>
> Methane/Landfill Gas Production Workers

Governmental and Regulatory Administration

This industry sector covers activities by public and private organizations associated with conservation and pollution prevention, regulation enforcement, and policy analysis and advocacy.

The change to a green economy will be more drastic, in some ways, than the change to the high-tech economy was. Businesses and individuals will have to learn new skills and will have to look at costs in new ways. To get there, they will need a mixture of education, persuasion, and government mandates.

For example, the conservation of our wildernesses and wildlife has been encouraged by a mixture of government dictates such as the establishment of the national park system, laws such as those regulating hunting and fishing, private purchases of land by conservation-minded citizens, advocacy groups such as the Sierra Club and Ducks Unlimited, and public education campaigns such as the Smokey the Bear advertisements.

Governmental and regulatory administration requires law enforcement officers, park administrators, pollution-control inspectors, and many other skilled workers. Here are some of the green occupations in this industry sector:

> Conservation Scientists and Foresters
>
> Construction and Building Inspectors
>
> Engineers
>
> Urban and Regional Planners

Key Points: Step 2

- Many industries are involved in the transition to a green economy.

- Within each industry, a diverse mix of workers is needed.

- You may be able to make a rewarding career in a green industry that interests you.

 STEP 3: Match Your Interests to Green Jobs

In Step 2, you read about the many different kinds of work being done in 12 industry sectors that are creating the green economy. If you're interested in one or more of these industries, it would be a good idea to narrow down your choices. What specific occupations might be good choices for you?

Think About Your Interests

One way to find a satisfying job is to clarify what interests you. It's not the only thing you should consider, of course. You want to get paid well enough and work in an environment that feels comfortable to you. But if you're like most people, it's very important that you stay interested in what you're doing for a living. You should enjoy dealing with the kinds of tasks and problems you encounter on the job.

People who write about careers have developed many ways to think about interests, but one of the simplest ways is to break them down into three very large areas: **Data, People,** and **Things.** These are terms that everybody understands, and they are a useful way of making a first cut of the world of work.

Most people have a certain amount of interest in all three of these large fields, and most jobs involve a mixture of all three. But you probably prefer one more than the other two, and in most jobs one dominates over the other two. So next you're going to do a quick exercise to help you decide which is your number-one interest, which is number two, and which is number three. Then you'll see which green jobs match your *Data-People-Things interest profile* or come close to it. (This exercise is an adaptation of one that was developed by the Delta College Career Services Office and is used with their permission.)

The psychology of interests is not an exact science, and the exercise that follows is not a scientific instrument. Nevertheless, it should give you insights that will help you understand which kinds of work might suit you best. Use common sense to combine the results of this exercise with other information you can get about yourself and your work options. Talk to people who know you and are familiar with your school and work experiences.

The exercise is easy to do—just follow the directions beginning with Step 3A. This is not a test, so there are no right or wrong answers and no time limit.

Step 3A: Respond to the Statements

Starting in the following box, carefully read each work activity (items 1 through 54). If you think you would LIKE to do the activity, circle the number of the activity. Don't consider whether you have the education or training needed for it or how much money you might earn if it were part of your job. Simply decide whether you would like the activity. If you know you would dislike the activity or you're not sure, leave the number unmarked.

After you respond to all 54 activities, you'll score your responses in Step 3B.

Circle the numbers of the activities you would LIKE to do.

1. Work with calculators and computers to solve math problems.

2. Read graphs or tables to answer questions or study a blueprint.

3. Sort things and put them in their proper place, like working in a library.

4. Perform math problems accurately, such as figuring the price of an item.

5. Measure things by reading scales or rulers, such as weighing meat or measuring cloth.

6. Get or give information, such as reporting for a newspaper or programming a computer.

7. Coordinate and manage the work of others, such as telling pilots when to land an airplane, telling someone how to make something, or scheduling a project.

8. Design and draw plans for things such as buildings, machines, or electrical systems.

(continued)

(continued)

9. Look for evidence to solve problems, such as diagnosing a disease or solving a crime.

10. Investigate and explore the nature of the world through such areas as chemistry, forestry, ecology, or biology.

11. Remember numbers or memorize information.

12. Develop a budget for an office, company, or project.

13. Take inventory of supplies in a pantry or pharmacy.

14. Inspect a store or supermarket.

15. Compare prices in a store or catalog and make purchases.

16. Research a topic in the library, organize the information, and write a report.

17. Work with statistics as part of a study.

18. Keep financial records and files.

____ **Score for Data**

Circle the numbers of the activities you would LIKE to do.

19. Take requests from and serve people, such as customers in a restaurant or passengers on an airplane.

20. Make people comfortable and safe, such as helping children cross the street or caring for the elderly.

21. Amuse people by performing in a skit or play.

22. Confront people who break rules, such as arresting someone who has broken the law or correcting students at school.

23. Instruct people, such as teaching children at school or training new workers.

24. Sell things to people, such as car insurance or a new project.

25. Help other people make decisions and solve problems, such as about how to diet, how to get money when they lose their job, or which trip to take.

26. Treat or care for sick people in a hospital.

27. Help handicapped persons do such things as learning to walk, read, or talk.

28. Counsel and listen to people with emotional difficulties.

29. Guide and advise people about legal, financial, family, or spiritual matters.

30. Work with a committee to decide on a new city program or solve a labor dispute.

31. Coach an athletic team or tutor students.

32. Supervise a group of people in an office.

33. Influence someone to buy a new appliance or real estate.

34. Entertain a group of government officials.

35. Explain things to people, such as the meaning of a historic site.

36. Convince people to accept your opinions about subjects such as politics or the news.

____ **Score for People**

Circle the numbers of the activities you would LIKE to do.

37. Mix things together to make something such as bread or cement.

38. Put parts together to build or make things such as furniture, gardens, or brick walls.

39. Use machines and tools to repair things such as light switches or broken windows.

40. Drive and operate heavy equipment such as a bulldozer, tractor, or truck.

41. Work with hand tools such as a saw, hammer, or screwdriver to make or repair things.

42. Keep things in good working order by checking or repairing things such as cars, airplanes, or televisions.

43. Follow plans to make things such as houses, books, or jewelry.

(continued)

44. Treat or care for animals.

45. Do skilled artistic work such as drawing cartoons, designing clothes, or painting pictures.

46. Develop and use special skills for working with materials such as sewing clothes, cutting hair, or cooking meals.

47. Fix computer equipment or medical testing machines.

48. Play a musical instrument.

49. Invent a new machine or design a new house.

50. Monitor equipment such as tape recorders or dials in a power plant.

51. Use scientific equipment to run laboratory tests.

52. Drive or operate a vehicle such as a car, bus, boat, or airplane.

53. Unload supplies for a stock room.

54. Feed and empty automatic machines.

____ **Score for Things**

Step 3B: Score Your Responses

Do the following to score your responses:

1. **Score the responses in each box.** In each box of responses, go from top to bottom and count how many numbers you circled. Then write that total on the "Score" line at the end of the box. Go on to the next box and do the same there.

2. **Determine your primary interest area.** Which Score has the highest number: **Data, People,** or **Things?** Enter the name of that interest on the following line.

My Primary Interest: _____

You will use your Primary Interest first to explore careers. (If two Scores are tied for the highest or are within 5 points of each other, use both of them for your Primary Interest. You are equally divided between two interests.)

3. **Determine your second and third interest areas.** Which Score has your next highest score? Which has your third highest score? Enter the names of those two interests on the following lines.

My Second Interest: _____

My Third Interest: _____

If you do not find many occupations that you like using your Primary Interest, you can use your Second Interest to look at more career options. Your Third Interest may help you identify choices that you want to avoid.

Step 3C: Find Jobs That Suit Your Interests

Start with your Primary Interest. In the following list, find the job titles that have your Primary Interest as their first interest field. Next, among these, look for jobs that have your Second Interest as their second interest field. You may find some job titles that are an exact match for all three elements of your interest profile, but also consider some jobs in which the second and third interests are not a perfect match.

Note to readers who have People as their Primary Interest: Only one job on the list has People as its top interest. Don't limit your thinking to this one job title; also look for jobs that have People as their second interest.

Circle the job titles that interest you. Don't rule out a job just because the title is not familiar to you.

Then turn to Step 5. The job descriptions there are listed alphabetically, so they're easy to find. When you're reading the job descriptions, focus especially on the educational or training requirements for the job, because that's what you're going to think about in the next chapter, Step 4.

Data-People-Things

Architects, Except Landscape and Naval

Biological Scientists

Computer Systems Analysts

Conservation Scientists and Foresters

Construction and Building Inspectors

Construction Managers

Energy Auditors

Engineering and Natural Sciences Managers

Engineers

Environmental Restoration Planners

Environmental Scientists and Specialists

Geoscientists and Hydrologists

Industrial Ecologists

Landscape Architects

Physicists

Surveyors, Cartographers, Photogrammetrists, and Surveying and Mapping Technicians

Urban and Regional Planners

Water Resource Specialists

Data-Things-People

Biofuels Production Workers

Biomass Energy Production Workers

Brownfield Redevelopment Specialists and Site Managers

Chemists and Materials Scientists

Drafters

Engineering Technicians

Fuel Cell Technicians

Geothermal Energy Production Workers

Hydroelectric Energy Production Workers

Methane/Landfill Gas Production Workers

Science Technicians

Solar Energy Production Workers

Wind Energy Production Workers

People-Things-Data

First-Line Supervisors/Managers of Construction Trades and Extraction Workers

Things-Data-People

Boilermakers

Electrical and Electronics Repairers, Powerhouse, Substation, and Relay

Electricians

Farmers, Ranchers, and Agricultural Managers

Forest and Conservation Workers

Hazardous Materials Removal Workers

Heating, Air-Conditioning, and Refrigeration Mechanics and Installers

Industrial Machinery Mechanics and Millwrights

Line Installers and Repairers

Plumbers, Pipelayers, Pipefitters, and Steamfitters

Power Plant Operators, Distributors, and Dispatchers

Sheet Metal Workers

Water and Liquid Waste Treatment Plant and System Operators

Weatherization Installers and Technicians

Welding, Soldering, and Brazing Workers

Things-People-Data

Carpenters

Construction Laborers

Glaziers

Insulation Workers

Roofers

Key Points: Step 3

- You're likely to get more satisfaction from a job if the work tasks and problems interest you.

- One handy way to think about your interests is in terms of Data, People, and Things.

- Occupations can be classified according to how much they involve Data, People, and Things, so you can find some that fit your interest profile (or come close to it).

STEP 4: Qualify for Green Jobs

Now that you've completed the exercise in Step 3, you should have a clearer idea of which green jobs might satisfy your interests. But employers don't simply throw their doors open for everybody who's interested in a job. They expect job applicants to have a background with the right combination of education, training, and work experience. That means that you have to prepare appropriately for any job you're considering.

Maybe you don't want to spend many long years preparing for career entry. That's okay, because the skill levels needed for green jobs vary greatly.

Although some require a college degree, many others require only a few weeks of on-the-job training.

In this chapter, you'll look at three levels of skill and see the green careers that are appropriate at each level. These are the three levels:

- On-the-job training

- Some work experience or a postsecondary program that takes two years or less

- A bachelor's degree or higher

Very few occupations have rigid entry requirements. That's especially true for many green occupations that are still emerging or changing rapidly. Sometimes you can enter these with less than the usual level of preparation. On the other hand, in rapidly changing fields, skill levels are often rising rapidly, and your opportunities may be limited if you have only the minimal level of preparation.

In general, your best bet is to get as much education or training as you can. The advantages of a college education—in terms of lifetime earnings and job security—are higher now than ever. The same applies to careers that require training rather than college: A long-term program will reap much higher rewards than a shorter program that teaches you only a limited set of skills and work habits.

Also, get used to the idea that you will probably need to continue learning new things throughout your working life, especially in the fast-moving green economy.

On-the-Job Training

Of the 50 jobs included in this book, 22 can be learned through on-the-job training. The U.S. Department of Labor assigns occupations to three levels of on-the-job training, as follows:

- **Short-term on-the-job training:** It is possible to work in these occupations and achieve an average level of performance within a few days or weeks through on-the-job training.

- **Moderate-term on-the-job training:** Occupations requiring this type of training can be performed adequately after a one- to twelve-month period of combined on-the-job and informal training.

- **Long-term on-the-job training:** This training requires more than 12 months of on-the-job training or combined work experience and formal classroom instruction. This includes occupations that use formal apprenticeships for training workers that may take up to four years.

Getting On-the-Job Training

Many workers get informal on-the-job training after being hired by an employer who recognizes that the worker is interested in the work, has a good attitude, and is able to learn. The employer then assigns this person to work alongside an experienced worker who can show the new recruit how to do the work tasks. In some situations, the employer may provide a training video or a computer-based lesson that covers some of the work skills.

A more formal version of this kind of training is an *apprenticeship.* Two things make an apprenticeship formal: One is the agreement that the apprentice signs with the employer, setting out the requirements that both parties must meet; the other is the nationally recognized credential that the apprentice gets after completing the program.

At worksites, skilled workers teach apprentices how to perform tasks at increasing levels of skill, and apprentices are rotated through all aspects of the job so that they learn the full range of skills. To learn concepts that cannot be taught well at the worksite—for example, technical math or principles of mechanics—apprentices take classes after working hours, often at a community college or a vocational school, by correspondence, or even on the Web. Apprentices earn while they learn. They start out at a rate of pay that is often only half the hourly rate of a fully qualified worker, but as they gain work experience they get regular increases in pay.

On-the-job training doesn't have to end once you learn the skills for an entry-level job. If you want to advance in a job or move into a different job, you may find it useful to start your own informal program for improving your skills. When you see co-workers using skills that you don't have, ask them to show you how. When you feel you have mastered the skill, ask your supervisor for an assignment that uses the skill—perhaps not a high-stakes project, but something that will demonstrate your new skill. Then be sure to ask for feedback that specifically targets your use of the skill. What did you do right? How could you have done it better? Try not to be defensive in response to criticism; use this feedback as part of the learning process.

If you're not working now, you can get informal on-the-job training in specific skills by doing volunteer work in a relevant setting. For example, to improve your people skills, do volunteer work at a senior center or a charity fund-raising event. Some hobbies also provide opportunities for you to learn skills—for example, designing Web pages, rock climbing, or gardening. With hobbies, it helps to join a club so you can learn from more highly skilled hobbyists and get feedback on your accomplishments. Just keep in mind that your volunteer work can do more than just help others and your hobby can be more than just a self-indulgence. Use them as skill academies, and then find ways to transfer those skills to your career.

Sometimes you can create your own training program by studying a book or technical manual. In fact, if the skill you want to learn is very rare (for example, carving stone) or on the leading edge of technology (for example, using the very latest software program), you may have no choice but to design your own curriculum because you can't find anyone to teach you. If you're very lucky, you may be able to convince your employer to pay for the books or other learning aids and to give you time in the workday for upgrading your skills. But most workers find that they have to use lunch hours, evenings, and weekends for this self-training. Consider the time and expense of self-training as investments in your future employability.

Try to find a study partner to learn with you; study partners help reinforce each other's learning and keep the learning program on track. Without a study partner, you're more likely to give up quickly.

Green Jobs That Usually Require On-the-Job Training

The following list shows green jobs that workers can learn through on-the-job training. (Some titles appear under more than one heading because the job may be entered at more than one level of skill.)

Short-term on-the-job training

Biomass Energy Production Workers

Plumbers, Pipelayers, Pipefitters, and Steamfitters

Weatherization Installers and Technicians

Moderate-term on-the-job training

Construction Laborers

Energy Auditors

Forest and Conservation Workers

Hazardous Materials Removal Workers

Industrial Machinery Mechanics and Millwrights

Insulation Workers

Roofers

Solar Energy Production Workers

Surveyors, Cartographers, Photogrammetrists, and Surveying and Mapping Technicians

Long-term on-the-job training

> Biomass Energy Production Workers
>
> Boilermakers
>
> Carpenters
>
> Electricians
>
> Farmers, Ranchers, and Agricultural Managers
>
> Glaziers
>
> Industrial Machinery Mechanics and Millwrights
>
> Line Installers and Repairers
>
> Plumbers, Pipelayers, Pipefitters, and Steamfitters
>
> Power Plant Operators, Distributors, and Dispatchers
>
> Sheet Metal Workers
>
> Stationary Engineers and Boiler Operators
>
> Water and Liquid Waste Treatment Plant and System Operators

Work Experience and Postsecondary Programs That Take Two Years or Less

Many green careers require more preparation than on-the-job training but less than four years of college. The U.S. Department of Labor defines three levels of preparation within this range, as follows:

- **Work experience in a related occupation:** Workers are expected to have learned certain skills in a related occupation.

- **Postsecondary vocational training:** This training requirement can vary from a few months to usually less than one year. In a few instances, as many as four years of training may be required.

- **Associate degree:** This degree usually requires two years of full-time academic work beyond high school.

Getting Work Experience in a Related Occupation

In some industries, a common way to get ahead is to use your experience in one occupation as your entry ticket to a related higher-level occupation.

For example, experienced construction workers—carpenters, electricians, or plumbers—may become crew chiefs if they have some leadership skills. Some eventually become owners of businesses employing many workers and may spend most of their time as managers rather than as craftsworkers. Others become building inspectors. From their work experience in construction, they gain knowledge of building codes. After some additional formal or informal studying, they pass the exam that gets them licensed or certified as an inspector.

This entry route is particularly useful for green jobs that are so new that formal educational and training programs have not yet been developed or are hard to find. For example, some of the technicians who service wind-powered or hydroelectric turbines enter their jobs after getting work experience repairing electric generators in other settings.

No matter what green job interests you, you should talk to workers in that occupation and find out how they qualified for their present position. You may find that many of them used work experience as their entry route, and this may be a practical route for you to follow, especially if formal preparation programs do not yet exist.

Getting Postsecondary Vocational Training

Many employers value the training that you can get at a postsecondary vocational school. Some of these schools are public institutions; others are private technical schools (or "institutes"). These training programs vary in length from a few weeks to two years and focus exclusively on job-related skills. Before you sign up for any program of this kind, especially if you need to borrow money to pay for it, you should check with local employers and with people who have completed the program. Make sure that the program has a good reputation with employers and is keeping up to date with changing workplace technologies.

Military training and the work experience that comes with it can be relevant to several green jobs. The armed forces are committed to reducing their energy consumption and therefore are training their personnel in conservation and in the use of green energy resources. Many of the well-established military occupations, such as those in construction and computer technologies, can give you work experience that you can apply to green jobs.

This entry route allows you to earn as you learn, serve your country, and get educational benefits that you can use after you re-enter civilian life. The military also teaches more than just the technical skills that are necessary to get the job done. People who have served in the military often mention several other skills and work-related attitudes they learn that serve them well throughout their career, such as teamwork, initiative, and a sense of responsibility.

Of course, signing up for the military means a commitment of several years and the loss of some freedoms. In practical terms, that means that you don't have the right to disobey lawful orders, tell your boss to take a hike, show up late for work, or quit. Remember also that the core business of the military is defense, which sometimes can require combat. Even training exercises can be dangerous. The risks to life and limb are real. On the other hand, many of the basic requirements of life are provided for you while you are on active duty. Most important, you not only get a job, but all the training you need for the job, and you are encouraged to get additional training to build your skills.

Enrolling in an Associate Degree Program

A bachelor's degree does open doors. But many people find happiness in jobs that require only an associate degree obtained through two years of study at a community college, junior college, technical college, or—in some cases—a college that also offers four-year degrees.

Associate degree programs often allow you to take classes either by day or in the evenings. Some classes may be available online or by correspondence, but many jobs involve some skills that you need to learn in person. If you take courses part time, earning your associate degree may take longer than two years.

The colleges usually try to match their programs to the needs of local employers. That means that two-year colleges are often the first to offer preparation programs for emerging green careers. It also means that the college—if it is good—is likely to have a good reputation with local employers. Before you sign up for a program, find out about job placement of recent graduates. Better yet, phone the human resources office of a local employer and ask whether they have hired graduates of the program—or whether there's another program that's better.

Green Jobs That Usually Require Work Experience or a Postsecondary Program That Takes Two Years or Less

Workers can learn the following green jobs with more preparation than on-the-job training but less than four years of college:

Work experience in a related occupation

> Construction and Building Inspectors
>
> First-Line Supervisors/Managers of Construction Trades and Extraction Workers
>
> Geothermal Energy Production Workers
>
> Hydroelectric Energy Production Workers
>
> Industrial Production Managers

Methane/Landfill Gas Production Workers

Wind Energy Production Workers

Postsecondary vocational training

Biofuels Production Workers

Drafters

Electrical and Electronics Repairers, Powerhouse, Substation, and Relay

Heating, Air-Conditioning, and Refrigeration Mechanics and Installers

Welding, Soldering, and Brazing Workers

Associate degree

Engineering Technicians

Fuel Cell Technicians

Science Technicians

Solar Energy Production Workers

Weatherization Installers and Technicians

Wind Energy Production Workers

Bachelor's Degree or Higher

A bachelor's degree can provide you with many advantages in the job market. Although most green jobs don't require it in the same way that it's required for teacher certification, many employers strongly prefer job candidates who have a bachelor's degree, sometimes in a specific major. In some green careers, additional work experience or a postgraduate degree is required or expected.

The U.S. Department of Labor defines four levels of preparation at the level of a bachelor's degree or higher, as follows:

- **Bachelor's degree:** This degree requires approximately four to five years of full-time academic work beyond high school.

- **Work experience plus degree:** Jobs in this category are often management-related and require some experience in a related nonmanagerial position.

- **Master's degree:** Completion of a master's degree usually requires one to two years of full-time study beyond the bachelor's degree.

- **Doctoral degree:** This degree normally requires two or more years of full-time academic work beyond the bachelor's degree.

Enrolling in a Program That Leads to a Bachelor's Degree or Higher

People who hold a bachelor's degree earn about one-third more than the average for all workers, and their unemployment rate is about one-third lower. A bachelor's degree is so valuable because it gives you a foundation for further learning. As our economy changes rapidly, especially in the green career field, workers will need to continue learning throughout their careers. Even workers who do not pursue higher-level degrees will need to take courses or pursue informal learning to remain productive as their jobs evolve. But continuous learning requires skills that go beyond the immediate demands of the job—skills in critical thinking, writing, math, and research methods. That's a major reason why employers prefer bachelor's degree holders over people who have taken courses related only to the entry-level job.

The earnings and employability advantages are even greater, on average, for those who get a postgraduate degree or the right combination of a degree and work experience. But keep in mind that the advantages of higher education and specialization are true only on average; some people with credentials that should be impressive find that they are overqualified for some jobs that they apply for. When you have a particular career goal in mind, talk to employers about the level of preparation they are seeking in the workers they hire, and don't assume that more education is always better.

To climb each step of the higher-education ladder, you'll need to be appropriately prepared with required courses, a record of good grades, recommendation letters, and perhaps suitable scores on an entrance exam. Higher education also can be very expensive. Be very cautious about borrowing money for higher education; college debt can burden you for years. There are several ways to minimize your expenses:

- Take advanced placement courses in high school.
- Start at a community college.
- Go to an in-state public institution.
- Search for scholarships, grants, or (at the graduate level) fellowships or teaching assistantships.
- Take advantage of work-study programs.
- Avoid changing majors and adding to your years of college.

Green Jobs That Usually Require a Bachelor's Degree or Higher

Workers can learn the following green jobs with a bachelor's degree or higher:

Bachelor's degree

> Architects, Except Landscape and Naval
>
> Biological Scientists
>
> Brownfield Redevelopment Specialists and Site Managers
>
> Chemists and Materials Scientists
>
> Computer Systems Analysts
>
> Conservation Scientists and Foresters
>
> Construction Managers
>
> Energy Auditors
>
> Engineers
>
> Environmental Restoration Planners
>
> Landscape Architects
>
> Science Technicians
>
> Surveyors, Cartographers, Photogrammetrists, and Surveying and Mapping Technicians

Work experience plus degree

> Engineering and Natural Sciences Managers
>
> Farmers, Ranchers, and Agricultural Managers
>
> Water Resource Specialists

Master's degree

> Brownfield Redevelopment Specialists and Site Managers
>
> Environmental Restoration Planners
>
> Environmental Scientists and Specialists
>
> Geoscientists and Hydrologists
>
> Industrial Ecologists
>
> Urban and Regional Planners

Doctoral degree

> Biological Scientists
>
> Physicists

Key Points: Step 4

- You don't need a college degree to work in a green job; many green jobs are open to people with less education or training.

- Several job-preparation routes are pathways you may not have considered, such as apprenticeship, informal on-the-job training, or military training.

- On average, having more education, training, or work experience results in better income and more job security.

- Before signing up for an educational or training program, talk to employers and workers to learn about the reputation of the entry route you have in mind.

 STEP 5: Discover What You'd Do in 50 Green Jobs

This chapter features descriptions of 50 green jobs. They are a mix of the three kinds of green jobs described in Step 1. They represent 11 of the 12 green industry sectors described in Step 2. They are characterized by different mixes of Data, People, and Things, the interest fields that are the theme of Step 3. And they are open to people with many different levels of education and training, as explained in Step 4. With such a diverse collection of jobs, you're likely to find several that interest you.

Here are some important notes on how to read and interpret the job descriptions:

- Job descriptions are arranged in alphabetical order by job title.

- The economic information here represents national averages that apply across all industries. The green industries may pay more or less than these averages; earnings in your community may also vary from the averages.

- The information about knowledge/courses is derived from the O*NET database of the U.S. Department of Labor. This gives you an idea of what you would study in an academic or training program, although it does not identify names of specific programs. Information about Data, People, and Things is also based on O*NET data, with the exception of a few emerging occupations for which data is not yet available. For these, estimates were provided based on an understanding of the work activities.

- These job descriptions are only a small snapshot of information. Before committing to a career goal, you should explore jobs in greater depth. All of the jobs included here are described in greater detail in JIST's edition of the *Occupational Outlook Handbook*. When you get closer to a decision, be sure to talk to people who actually do the work.

■ Architects, Except Landscape and Naval.
Plan and design structures such as private residences, office buildings, theaters, factories, and other structural property.

Green Sector(s): Green Construction; Research, Design, and Consulting Services. **Role in the Green Economy:** Job prospects are expected to be favorable for architects with knowledge of green design (also known as sustainable design), which emphasizes energy efficiency; renewable resources; waste reduction; and environmentally friendly design, specifications, and materials.

Education/Training Required: Bachelor's degree. **Average Annual Earnings:** $72,700. **Growth Through 2018:** High. **Annual Job Openings:** 4,680.

Career Cluster(s): 02 Architecture and Construction. **Knowledge/Courses:** Design; Building and Construction; Engineering and Technology; Fine Arts; Sales and Marketing; Law and Government; Sociology and Anthropology; History and Archeology. **Interests:** Data—Very high, People—High, Things—Medium.

■ Biofuels Production Workers.
Operate, maintain, and manage facilities that produce useful fuels from plant matter.

Green Sector(s): Renewable Energy Generation. **Role in the Green Economy:** All biofuels generate carbon dioxide gas when they are burned, but the plants from which the biofuels are made absorb this gas from the atmosphere. This cycle of growth and combustion, which ultimately derives its energy from the sunlight that falls on green leaves, defines biofuels as a renewable source of energy.

Education/Training Required: Associate degree. **Average Annual Earnings:** $30,000–$70,000. **Growth Through 2018:** Probably very high. **Annual Job Openings:** No data available.

Career Cluster(s): 04 Business, Management, and Administration; 13 Manufacturing. **Knowledge/Courses:** No data available. **Interests:** Data—High, People—Medium, Things—High.

■ Biological Scientists.
Study living organisms and their relationship to the environment. Perform research to gain a better understanding of fundamental life processes or apply that understanding to developing new products or processes.

Green Sector(s): Environmental Protection. **Role in the Green Economy:** Biological scientists will be needed to determine the environmental impact of industry and government actions and to prevent or correct environmental problems such as the negative effects of pesticide use. Some biological scientists will find opportunities in environmental regulatory agencies, while others will use their expertise to advise lawmakers on legislation to save environmentally sensitive areas. New industrial applications of biotechnology, such as new methods for making ethanol for transportation fuel, also will spur demand for biological scientists.

Education/Training Required: Bachelor's degree; doctoral degree. **Average Annual Earnings:** $68,707. **Growth Through 2018:** Very high. **Annual Job Openings:** 4,860.

Career Cluster(s): 01 Agriculture, Food, and Natural Resources; 08 Health Science; 11 Information Technology; 15 Science, Technology, Engineering, and Mathematics. **Knowledge/Courses:** Biology; Chemistry; Medicine and Dentistry; English Language; Education and Training; Mathematics; Computers and Electronics; Physics. **Interests:** Data—High, People—Medium, Things—Medium.

■ **Biomass Energy Production Workers.** Operate, maintain, and manage facilities that generate energy from recently living organisms such as wood, agricultural residues, and waste paper.

Green Sector(s): Renewable Energy Generation. **Role in the Green Economy:** The plants that create biomass draw carbon dioxide from the air as they grow. Thus, even if burning biomass liberates carbon dioxide, the net effect is carbon-neutral. Some environmental scientists are concerned about particulates that are produced when biomass burns. They also warn against cutting down forests to obtain biomass. One especially green way to use biomass is to burn only feedstocks that are already concentrated in one place and would otherwise be wasted, such as rice hulls.

Education/Training Required: Short-term on-the-job training; long-term on-the-job training. **Average Annual Earnings:** $40,000–$60,000. **Growth Through 2018:** Probably high. **Annual Job Openings:** No data available.

Career Cluster(s): 04 Business, Management, and Administration; 13 Manufacturing. **Knowledge/Courses:** No data available. **Interests:** Data—High, People—Medium, Things—High.

■ **Boilermakers.** Construct, assemble, maintain, and repair stationary steam boilers and boiler house auxiliaries. Align structures or plate sections to assemble boiler frame tanks or vats, following blueprints. Work involves use of hand and power tools, plumb bobs, levels, wedges, dogs, or turnbuckles. Assist in testing assembled vessels. Direct cleaning of boilers and boiler furnaces.

Inspect and repair boiler fittings, such as safety valves, regulators, automatic-control mechanisms, water columns, and auxiliary machines.

Green Sector(s): Energy Efficiency; Green Construction. **Role in the Green Economy:** The Energy Policy Act of 2005 is expected to lead to the construction of many new clean-burning coal power plants, spurring demand for boilermakers. The law is designed to promote conservation and use of cleaner technologies in energy production through tax credits and higher efficiency standards. In addition, boilermakers will be needed for the construction of ethanol distilleries, geothermal power plants, and other facilities that produce energy from renewable sources.

Education/Training Required: Long-term on-the-job training. **Average Annual Earnings:** $56,100. **Growth Through 2018:** High. **Annual Job Openings:** 810.

Career Cluster(s): 02 Architecture and Construction. **Knowledge/Courses:** Building and Construction; Mechanical; Engineering and Technology; Design; Physics; Transportation; Production and Processing; Chemistry. **Interests:** Data—Medium, People—Medium, Things—Very high.

■ Brownfield Redevelopment Specialists and Site Managers.
Participate in planning and directing cleanup and redevelopment of contaminated properties for reuse. Does not include properties sufficiently contaminated to qualify as Superfund sites.

Green Sector(s): Green Construction; Recycling and Waste Reduction. **Role in the Green Economy:** Restoration of brownfields produces many environmental benefits. Cleaning up a site removes contaminants and prevents them from polluting surrounding areas. The recycling of land that has previously been developed reduces the need for sprawl. Brownfields are often located near urban cores or rail lines, where new commercial activity creates less additional automobile use. Redeveloped sites also tend to be more compact and thus produce less rainwater runoff.

Education/Training Required: Bachelor's degree; master's degree. **Average Annual Earnings:** No data available. **Growth Through 2018:** No data available. **Annual Job Openings:** No data available.

Career Cluster(s): 04 Business, Management, and Administration. **Knowledge/Courses:** No data available. **Interests:** Data—High, People—Medium, Things—High.

■ Carpenters.
Construct, erect, install, or repair structures and fixtures made of wood, such as concrete forms; building frameworks, including partitions, joists, studding, and rafters; wood stairways; window and door frames; and hardwood floors. May also install cabinets, siding, drywall, and batt or

roll insulation. Includes brattice builders who build doors or brattices (ventilation walls or partitions) in underground passageways to control the proper circulation of air through the passageways and to the working places.

Green Sector(s): Green Construction. **Role in the Green Economy:** The job of carpenter is not inherently green, but carpenters can specialize in projects related to green energy and conservation, such as installing heat-saving windows and doors or rehabilitating old buildings instead of tearing them down. Carpenters can also learn to use greener construction materials, such as recycled glass tiles. Learning these green techniques is not necessarily part of every apprenticeship or other training program; you have to take the initiative to learn about them.

Education/Training Required: Long-term on-the-job training. **Average Annual Earnings:** $39,470. **Growth Through 2018:** Average. **Annual Job Openings:** 32,540.

Career Cluster(s): 02 Architecture and Construction. **Knowledge/Courses:** Building and Construction; Design; Mechanical; Production and Processing; Engineering and Technology; Mathematics; Public Safety and Security; Administration and Management. **Interests:** Data—Low, People—Medium, Things—High.

■ **Chemists and Materials Scientists.** Conduct chemical analyses or chemical experiments in laboratories for quality or process control or to develop new products or knowledge.

Green Sector(s): Research, Design, and Consulting Services. **Role in the Green Economy:** Environmental research will offer many new opportunities for chemists and materials scientists. To satisfy public concerns and to comply with government regulations, chemical manufacturing industries will continue to invest billions of dollars each year in technology that reduces pollution and cleans up existing waste sites. Research into traditional and alternative energy sources should also lead to employment growth among chemists.

Education/Training Required: Bachelor's degree. **Average Annual Earnings:** $69,428. **Growth Through 2018:** Low. **Annual Job Openings:** 3,440.

Career Cluster(s): 15 Science, Technology, Engineering, and Mathematics. **Knowledge/Courses:** Chemistry; Engineering and Technology; Physics; Mathematics; Production and Processing; Clerical; Computers and Electronics; Administration and Management. **Interests:** Data—Medium, People—Low, Things—Medium.

■ **Computer Systems Analysts.** Analyze science, engineering, business, and all other data processing problems for application to electronic data processing systems. Analyze user requirements, procedures, and problems to automate or improve existing systems and review computer system capabilities, workflow, and scheduling limitations. May analyze or recommend commercially available software. May supervise computer programmers.

Green Sector(s): Energy Efficiency; Research, Design, and Consulting Services. **Role in the Green Economy:** Businesses and industries need good information if they want to function in a more green manner. A particularly noteworthy example is the nation's electric power grid. The key to the planned upgrade to a "smart" grid is information technology that will allow the grid to react instantaneously to changes in the availability and use of power. Systems analysts also help transportation companies to work out the most efficient route assignments of buses, trucks, and taxis.

Education/Training Required: Bachelor's degree. **Average Annual Earnings:** $77,080. **Growth Through 2018:** Very high. **Annual Job Openings:** 22,280.

Career Cluster(s): 08 Health Science; 11 Information Technology. **Knowledge/Courses:** Computers and Electronics; Engineering and Technology; Clerical; Education and Training; Design; Telecommunications; Customer and Personal Service; English Language. **Interests:** Data—High, People—High, Things—Medium.

■ **Conservation Scientists and Foresters.** Manage the use and development of forests, rangelands, and other natural resources.

Green Sector(s): Agriculture and Forestry; Environmental Protection; Governmental and Regulatory Administration. **Role in the Green Economy:** It's hard to imagine a greener work environment than the forest, and many people are attracted to these careers because of this setting. In the past, the forestry industry was similar to mining in that a resource was extracted once and then was gone. Nowadays, as timber is removed, new trees are planted. In addition, many foresters and conservation scientists are employed solely to conserve these green environments by controlling pests and taking actions to make fires less likely and easier to control. Urban foresters encourage a refreshing level of greenery in our cities.

Education/Training Required: Bachelor's degree. **Average Annual Earnings:** $57,769. **Growth Through 2018:** Average. **Annual Job Openings:** 680.

Career Cluster(s): 01 Agriculture, Food, and Natural Resources. **Knowledge/Courses:** Biology; Geography; History and Archeology; Building and Construction; Physics; Engineering and Technology; Law and Government; Food Production. **Interests:** Data—High, People—High, Things—Medium.

■ **Construction and Building Inspectors.** Inspect structures using engineering skills to determine structural soundness and compliance with specifications, building codes, and other regulations. Inspections may be general in nature or may be limited to a specific area, such as electrical systems or plumbing.

Green Sector(s): Governmental and Regulatory Administration; Green Construction. **Role in the Green Economy:** Construction and building inspectors are largely guided by codes and standards. New standards, such as LEED, are intended to encourage greener building practices. Inspectors can obtain various levels and specializations of LEED certification, as well as training programs that prepare candidates for the certification exams, from the Green Building Certification Institute.

Education/Training Required: Work experience in a related occupation. **Average Annual Earnings:** $51,530. **Growth Through 2018:** High. **Annual Job Openings:** 3,970.

Career Cluster(s): 02 Architecture and Construction. **Knowledge/Courses:** Building and Construction; Engineering and Technology; Design; Physics; Public Safety and Security; Mechanical; Customer and Personal Service; Law and Government. **Interests:** Data—Medium, People—Medium, Things—Medium.

■ **Construction Laborers.** Perform tasks involving physical labor at building, highway, and heavy construction projects; tunnel and shaft excavations; and demolition sites. May operate hand and power tools of all types: air hammers, earth tampers, cement mixers, small mechanical hoists, surveying and measuring equipment, and a variety of other equipment and instruments. May clean and prepare sites; dig trenches; set braces to support the sides of excavations; erect scaffolding; clean up rubble and debris; and remove asbestos, lead, and other hazardous waste materials. May assist other craft workers.

Green Sector(s): Green Construction. **Role in the Green Economy:** Construction laborers are needed for many projects that make our economy more sustainable. It is possible to specialize in green construction, especially by working for a contractor who focuses on green projects. Every geothermal power plant or biofuels production facility starts as a construction effort. The construction industry also uses laborers in environmental remediation projects. While doing this kind of work, you may be offered training as a hazardous materials removal worker.

Education/Training Required: Moderate-term on-the-job training. **Average Annual Earnings:** $29,150. **Growth Through 2018:** Very high. **Annual Job Openings:** 33,940.

Career Cluster(s): 02 Architecture and Construction. **Knowledge/Courses:** Building and Construction; Design; Mechanical; Transportation; Public Safety and Security; Engineering and Technology; Physics; Production and Processing. **Interests:** Data—Very low, People—Low, Things—High.

■ **Construction Managers.** Plan, direct, coordinate, or budget, usually through subordinate supervisory personnel, activities concerned with the construction and maintenance of structures, facilities, and systems. Participate in the conceptual development of a construction project and oversee its organization, scheduling, and implementation.

Green Sector(s): Environmental Protection; Green Construction. **Role in the Green Economy:** Construction managers interested in green practices now have many recycled materials available for use. Some constructors specialize in rehabilitating buildings, turning abandoned factories into office spaces and old row houses into modern, energy-efficient apartments. Others specialize in green building features such as a roof covered with green plantings, windows that maximize heat gain and light from sunshine, and subfloor spaces that circulate warm air more efficiently than traditional ducts.

Education/Training Required: Bachelor's degree. **Average Annual Earnings:** $82,330. **Growth Through 2018:** High. **Annual Job Openings:** 13,770.

Career Cluster(s): 02 Architecture and Construction; 04 Business, Management, and Administration. **Knowledge/Courses:** Building and Construction; Design; Engineering and Technology; Mechanical; Administration and Management; Personnel and Human Resources; Economics and Accounting; Public Safety and Security. **Interests:** Data—Very high, People—High, Things—Medium.

■ **Drafters.** Prepare technical drawings and plans, which are used to build everything from manufactured products such as toys, toasters, industrial machinery, and spacecraft to structures such as houses, office buildings, and oil and gas pipelines.

Green Sector(s): Green Construction. **Role in the Green Economy:** The shift to a green economy will create many opportunities for drafters. Architectural drafters will prepare drawings of renewable-energy power plants and energy-efficient buildings. Mechanical and electronic drafters will represent designs for new machines and high-tech devices for producing energy and using it more efficiently—including the plug-in electric cars of the future.

Education/Training Required: Postsecondary vocational training. **Average Annual Earnings:** $47,150. **Growth Through 2018:** Low. **Annual Job Openings:** 6,570.

Career Cluster(s): 02 Architecture and Construction; 15 Science, Technology, Engineering, and Mathematics. **Knowledge/Courses:** Design; Engineering and Technology; Building and Construction; Computers and Electronics; Physics; Mathematics; Mechanical; Production and Processing. **Interests:** Data—Medium, People—Low, Things—Medium.

▇ Electrical and Electronics Repairers, Powerhouse, Substation, and Relay.
Inspect, test, repair, or maintain electrical equipment in generating stations, substations, and in-service relays.

Green Sector(s): Renewable Energy Generation. **Role in the Green Economy:** The growth of green energy means powerhouses will be built in installations that use energy from solar heat, geothermal heat, and biomass-fired boilers. Powerhouses using nonrenewable energy resources will adopt new practices and technologies to conserve energy. Much of the increased demand for this occupation will be in these green sectors of the energy industry.

Education/Training Required: Postsecondary vocational training. **Average Annual Earnings:** $62,270. **Growth Through 2018:** Average. **Annual Job Openings:** 670.

Career Cluster(s): 13 Manufacturing. **Knowledge/Courses:** Mechanical; Design; Telecommunications; Building and Construction; Physics; Public Safety and Security. **Interests:** Data—High, People—Medium, Things—Very high.

▇ Electricians.
Install, maintain, and repair electrical wiring, equipment, and fixtures. Ensure that work is in accordance with relevant codes. May install or service street lights, intercom systems, or electrical control systems.

Green Sector(s): Green Construction. **Role in the Green Economy:** Some electricians specialize in installing solar photovoltaic systems, which generate power from sunlight and must be connected to the electrical wiring of the building consuming the power. Other electricians work in power plants that generate electricity from hydropower, hot rock formations, timber residues, or other sources of renewable energy. Wind turbines also need to be wired into the local power grid. Even green energy sources that don't generate electric power, such as biofuels production plants, use electricians to hook up machines and controls.

Education/Training Required: Long-term on-the-job training. **Average Annual Earnings:** $47,180. **Growth Through 2018:** Average. **Annual Job Openings:** 25,090.

Career Cluster(s): 02 Architecture and Construction. **Knowledge/ Courses:** Building and Construction; Mechanical; Design; Physics; Telecommunications; Engineering and Technology; Mathematics; Administration and Management. **Interests:** Data—Medium, People— Medium, Things—Very high.

■ **Energy Auditors.** Conduct energy audits of buildings, building systems, and process systems. May also conduct investment-grade audits of buildings or systems.

Green Sector(s): Energy Efficiency. **Role in the Green Economy:** It has often been said that the cheapest energy is the energy you don't use. Each megawatt of energy that is conserved means less oil being imported, less destruction of the landscape for coal extraction, and less fouling of the air with toxic fumes and greenhouse gases. Consumers and businesses can conserve energy only when they know where and how the energy is being wasted, and that's what energy auditors are trained to discover.

Education/Training Required: Moderate-term on-the-job training; bachelor's degree. **Average Annual Earnings:** $40,000–$80,000. **Growth Through 2018:** Probably very high. **Annual Job Openings:** No data available.

Career Cluster(s): 04 Business, Management, and Administration. **Knowledge/Courses:** Building and Construction; Physics; Sales and Marketing; Design; Clerical; Mechanical. **Interests:** Data—High, People— Medium, Things—Medium.

■ **Engineering and Natural Sciences Managers.** Plan, coordinate, and direct research, design, and production activities.

Green Sector(s): Environmental Protection; Renewable Energy Generation; Research, Design, and Consulting Services. **Role in the Green Economy:** The transition to a green economy will employ many managers for projects doing scientific research and engineering development. For example, before it becomes practical to create diesel fuel from algae, scientists will need to identify the most promising species and understand what growing conditions are most favorable for them. Next, engineers will need to develop efficient processes for growing and harvesting these algae and for transforming their oily substances into diesel-ready fuel.

Education/Training Required: Bachelor's or higher degree plus experience. **Average Annual Earnings:** $116,515. **Growth Through 2018:** Average. **Annual Job Openings:** 6,880.

Career Cluster(s): 02 Architecture and Construction; 04 Business, Management, and Administration; 08 Health Science; 11 Information Technology; 15 Science, Technology, Engineering, and Mathematics.

Knowledge/Courses: Engineering and Technology; Physics; Design; Chemistry; Building and Construction; Mathematics; Administration and Management; Computers and Electronics. **Interests:** Data—High, People—High, Things—Medium.

▓ **Engineering Technicians.** Use the principles and theories of science, engineering, and mathematics to solve technical problems in research and development, manufacturing, sales, construction, inspection, and maintenance.

Green Sector(s): Environmental Protection; Manufacturing; Research, Design, and Consulting Services; Transportation. **Role in the Green Economy:** Environmental engineering technicians help keep our environment clean. They sample and analyze surface and ground waters, help install and operate electronic equipment used to monitor air and water contaminants, assist in the cleanup of hazardous spills, and participate in the inspection of regulated facilities. Other kinds of engineering technicians are helping to design materials, machinery, roads, industrial processes, and consumer products that conserve energy or recycle materials.

Education/Training Required: Associate degree. **Average Annual Earnings:** $51,174. **Growth Through 2018:** Low. **Annual Job Openings:** 12,480.

Career Cluster(s): 01 Agriculture, Food, and Natural Resources; 02 Architecture and Construction; 13 Manufacturing; 15 Science, Technology, Engineering, and Mathematics; 16 Transportation, Distribution, and Logistics. **Knowledge/Courses:** Engineering and Technology; Design; Mechanical; Physics; Computers and Electronics; Production and Processing; Mathematics; Building and Construction. **Interests:** Data—Medium, People—Medium, Things—Medium.

▓ **Engineers.** Use scientific and mathematical principles to create products, improve processes, and solve problems.

Green Sector(s): Energy Efficiency; Environmental Protection; Governmental and Regulatory Administration; Green Construction; Manufacturing; Renewable Energy Generation; Research, Design, and Consulting Services; Transportation. **Role in the Green Economy:** Many of the best-paying jobs in renewable energy production will be for engineers who develop new processes, research ways to improve existing processes, design facilities, and consult during construction and start-up of new facilities. In addition, engineers are finding greener ways to accomplish traditional projects, such as constructing highways with recycled materials, designing buildings for greater heat efficiency, and redesigning industrial processes to capture and utilize waste heat and byproducts.

Education/Training Required: Bachelor's degree. **Average Annual Earnings:** $82,632. **Growth Through 2018:** Average. **Annual Job Openings:** 53,170.

Career Cluster(s): 02 Architecture and Construction; 08 Health Science; 11 Information Technology; 15 Science, Technology, Engineering, and Mathematics. **Knowledge/Courses:** Engineering and Technology; Design; Physics; Mechanical; Chemistry; Mathematics; Building and Construction; Computers and Electronics. **Interests:** Data—High, People—Medium, Things—Medium.

■ **Environmental Restoration Planners.** Collaborate with field and biology staff to oversee the implementation of restoration projects and to develop new products. Process and synthesize complex scientific data into practical strategies for restoration, monitoring, or management.

Green Sector(s): Environmental Protection. **Role in the Green Economy:** Because we are surrounded by natural ecosystems, the health of our environment affects human health. The work of environmental restoration planners rehabilitates damaged or degraded ecosystems, making the world greener. Environmental restoration planners may not be able to reverse the largest-scale environmental stressors, such as global warming, but they are often able to restore vitality to small-scale ecosystems, such as forest tracts, lakes, or wetlands.

Education/Training Required: Bachelor's degree; master's degree. **Average Annual Earnings:** No data available. **Growth Through 2018:** No data available. **Annual Job Openings:** No data available.

Career Cluster(s): 01 Agriculture, Food, and Natural Resources. **Knowledge/ Courses:** No data available. **Interests:** Data—High, People—Medium, Things—Medium.

■ **Environmental Scientists and Specialists.** Use their knowledge of the natural sciences to protect the environment by identifying problems and finding solutions that minimize hazards to the health of the environment and the population.

Green Sector(s): Environmental Protection. **Role in the Green Economy:** Environmental scientists and hydrologists will be in demand because of the need to monitor the quality of the environment, to interpret the impact of human actions on terrestrial and aquatic ecosystems, and to develop strategies for restoring ecosystems. In addition, environmental scientists will be needed to help planners develop and construct buildings, transportation corridors, and utilities that protect water resources and reflect efficient and beneficial land use.

Education/Training Required: Master's degree. **Average Annual Earnings:** $61,010. **Growth Through 2018:** Very high. **Annual Job Openings:** 4,840.

Career Cluster(s): 01 Agriculture, Food, and Natural Resources. **Knowledge/ Courses:** Biology; Geography; Chemistry; Physics; Law and Government; Engineering and Technology; Mathematics; English Language. **Interests:** Data—High, People—Medium, Things—Medium.

Farmers, Ranchers, and Agricultural Managers. Direct activities on farms and other agricultural establishments.

Green Sector(s): Agriculture and Forestry. **Role in the Green Economy:** Agricultural managers are adopting new practices to make their farms and ranches more energy-efficient and sustainable. For example, organic farming and integrated pest management are permitting smaller inputs of artificial fertilizers and pesticides. No-till farming reduces the energy demands of plowing and preserves soil structure. Livestock feedlot managers are learning how to use anaerobic digesters to convert manure to useful fertilizer while producing methane gas, a fuel resource. Meanwhile, consumers are finding ways to buy from local farms. This movement has improved the outlook for farms near cities and suburbs.

Education/Training Required: Long-term on-the-job training; bachelor's or higher degree plus experience. **Average Annual Earnings:** $55,712. **Growth Through 2018:** Declining. **Annual Job Openings:** 12,520.

Career Cluster(s): 01 Agriculture, Food, and Natural Resources. **Knowledge/ Courses:** Food Production; Biology; Sales and Marketing; Building and Construction; Economics and Accounting; Chemistry; Production and Processing; Geography. **Interests:** Data—Medium, People—Medium, Things—High.

First-Line Supervisors/Managers of Construction Trades and Extraction Workers. Directly supervise and coordinate activities of construction or extraction workers.

Green Sector(s): Green Construction. **Role in the Green Economy:** As engineers develop greener ways to do construction and extract resources from the ground, first-line supervisors will train laborers and tradesworkers in the new practices and technologies. Likewise, as new standards are imposed by law, these supervisors will ensure that workers adhere to them.

Education/Training Required: Work experience in a related occupation. **Average Annual Earnings:** $58,330. **Growth Through 2018:** High. **Annual Job Openings:** 24,220.

Career Cluster(s): 02 Architecture and Construction. **Knowledge/ Courses:** Building and Construction; Mechanical; Design; Engineering and

Technology; Production and Processing; Public Safety and Security. **Interests:** Data—High, People—Medium, Things—High.

■ **Forest and Conservation Workers.** Under supervision, perform manual labor necessary to develop, maintain, or protect forest, forested areas, and woodlands through such activities as raising and transporting tree seedlings; combating insects, pests, and diseases harmful to trees; and building structures to control water flow, erosion, and leaching of forest soil. Includes forester aides, seedling pullers, and tree planters.

Green Sector(s): Agriculture and Forestry; Environmental Protection. **Role in the Green Economy:** Demand for forest and conservation workers will increase as more land is set aside to protect natural resources or wildlife habitats. In addition, more jobs may be created by recent federal legislation designed to prevent destructive wildfires by thinning the forests and by setting controlled burns in dry regions susceptible to forest fires.

Education/Training Required: Moderate-term on-the-job training. **Average Annual Earnings:** $25,580. **Growth Through 2018:** Average. **Annual Job Openings:** 450.

Career Cluster(s): 01 Agriculture, Food, and Natural Resources. **Knowledge/ Courses:** Geography; Biology; History and Archeology; Transportation; Mechanical; Production and Processing; Economics and Accounting; Mathematics. **Interests:** Data—Medium, People—Medium, Things—High.

■ **Fuel Cell Technicians.** Install, operate, and maintain integrated fuel cell systems in transportation, stationary, or portable applications.

Green Sector(s): Energy Efficiency. **Role in the Green Economy:** Fuel cells "burn" fuel more efficiently, cleanly, and quietly than most traditional power-generating technologies because they generate electricity without any actual combustion. As electric motors replace internal-combustion engines in cars and trucks, fuel cells are likely to provide an alternative to heavy and bulky storage batteries.

Education/Training Required: Associate degree. **Average Annual Earnings:** No data available. **Growth Through 2018:** No data available. **Annual Job Openings:** No data available.

Career Cluster(s): 13 Manufacturing. **Knowledge/Courses:** No data available. **Interests:** Data—High, People—Medium, Things—High.

■ **Geoscientists and Hydrologists.** Study the composition, structure, and other physical aspects of the Earth and the Earth's geologic past and present by using sophisticated instruments to analyze the composition of earth, rock, and water.

Green Sector(s): Environmental Protection; Research, Design, and Consulting Services. **Role in the Green Economy:** Although many geoscientists work in the oil and coal extraction industries, others are finding employment in green industries. For example, geoscientists are needed to monitor the quality of the environment, including aquatic ecosystems, deteriorating coastal environments, and rising sea levels—all activities that will create employment growth for this occupation. Geoscientists are also involved in studies of the environmental impact of planned construction.

Education/Training Required: Master's degree. **Average Annual Earnings:** $79,836. **Growth Through 2018:** High. **Annual Job Openings:** 1,920.

Career Cluster(s): 15 Science, Technology, Engineering, and Mathematics. **Knowledge/Courses:** Geography; Engineering and Technology; Physics; Chemistry; Design; Biology; Mathematics; Computers and Electronics. **Interests:** Data—High, People—Medium, Things—Medium.

■ **Geothermal Energy Production Workers.** Operate, maintain, and manage facilities that generate energy from heat within the Earth.

Green Sector(s): Renewable Energy Generation. **Role in the Green Economy:** Geothermal power generation has many advantages over traditional sources of energy and even over some green sources. It emits no combustion gases during operations. All U.S. geothermal plants use air cooling and thus dump no waste heat into waterways. They use less land per megawatt of power than plants using fossil fuels, nuclear reactors, sunshine, or wind. No fuel needs to be delivered to the sites, nor waste products taken away. The impact on wildlife is negligible. Power is available 365 days per year.

Education/Training Required: Work experience in a related occupation. **Average Annual Earnings:** $40,000–$60,000. **Growth Through 2018:** Probably very high. **Annual Job Openings:** No data available.

Career Cluster(s): 04 Business, Management, and Administration; 13 Manufacturing. **Knowledge/Courses:** No data available. **Interests:** Data—High, People—Medium, Things—High.

■ **Glaziers.** Install glass in windows, skylights, store fronts, and display cases or on surfaces such as building fronts, interior walls, ceilings, and tabletops.

Green Sector(s): Green Construction; Manufacturing; Renewable Energy Generation. **Role in the Green Economy:** Many projects for making homes and buildings more energy-efficient require the work of glaziers. In the average house, around one-third of heat loss is through windows. Glaziers replace heat-leaking windows and sliding glass doors with high-tech upgrades. They also install windows or skylights to let in increased daylight and solar heat.

Although solar panels for electricity or heat are coated with glass, they usually are assembled at a factory, so glaziers are not involved. However, some glazing contractors also perform solar panel installations.

Education/Training Required: Long-term on-the-job training. **Average Annual Earnings:** $35,590. **Growth Through 2018:** Average. **Annual Job Openings:** 2,390.

Career Cluster(s): 02 Architecture and Construction. **Knowledge/ Courses:** Building and Construction; Mechanical; Design; Engineering and Technology; Mathematics; Public Safety and Security. **Interests:** Data—Very low, People—low, Things—Medium.

■ **Hazardous Materials Removal Workers.** Identify, remove, pack, transport, or dispose of hazardous materials, including asbestos, lead-based paint, waste oil, fuel, transmission fluid, radioactive materials, contaminated soil, and so on. Specialized training and certification in hazardous materials handling or a confined entry permit are generally required. May operate earth-moving equipment or trucks.

Green Sector(s): Environmental Protection; Green Construction; Recycling and Waste Reduction. **Role in the Green Economy:** The transition to a green economy will not necessarily mean fewer hazardous waste cleanups. New industries often create new hazards. For example, computers, cell phones, and other electronic equipment contain lead, mercury, cadmium, and brominated flame retardants, all of which end up in the waste stream of the manufacturing plants and in the landfills where old products are discarded. Nanotechnology, which creates new materials on a molecular scale, may lead to new ways to clean up wastes, but it is also creating new kinds of wastes with unknown risks. New regulations and new procedures for cleanup will need to be developed to deal with the byproducts of the green economy.

Education/Training Required: Moderate-term on-the-job training. **Average Annual Earnings:** $37,280. **Growth Through 2018:** High. **Annual Job Openings:** 1,780.

Career Cluster(s): 01 Agriculture, Food, and Natural Resources; 13 Manufacturing. **Knowledge/Courses:** Chemistry; Building and Construction; Mechanical; Transportation; Physics; Public Safety and Security; Medicine and Dentistry; Education and Training. **Interests:** Data—High, People—High, Things—Very high.

■ **Heating, Air-Conditioning, and Refrigeration Mechanics and Installers.** Set up or repair heating, central air-conditioning, or refrigeration systems.

Green Sector(s): Energy Efficiency; Green Construction. **Role in the Green Economy:** Because so much of America's energy use goes to heating and cooling homes and businesses, HVAC technicians have an important role to play in reducing energy consumption. Responding to this need, one of the skill-certifying organizations now offers an exam by which a technician can earn the title HVAC Efficiency Analyst. This title is meant to indicate a senior level of skills, so only those who have two other certifications may take the exam.

Education/Training Required: Postsecondary vocational training. **Average Annual Earnings:** $41,100. **Growth Through 2018:** Very high. **Annual Job Openings:** 13,620.

Career Cluster(s): 02 Architecture and Construction. **Knowledge/Courses:** Mechanical; Building and Construction; Physics; Chemistry; Design; Engineering and Technology; Sales and Marketing; Food Production. **Interests:** Data—Medium, People—Medium, Things—Very high.

■ **Hydroelectric Energy Production Workers.** Operate, maintain, and manage facilities that generate energy from the force of moving water.

Green Sector(s): Renewable Energy Generation. **Role in the Green Economy:** The most common form of hydropower, created by damming a river, is sometimes considered less "green" than other forms of renewable energy because of its environmental costs. The dam may obstruct fish migration, impede sediment flows, and deprive downstream wetlands of natural flooding. However, the process does not emit fumes or consume a nonrenewable resource, the technology is well established, and the power is reliable. Some experimental forms of hydropower, such as buoys that generate power from wave action, are expected to have the advantage of more benign environmental impact.

Education/Training Required: Work experience in a related occupation. **Average Annual Earnings:** $40,000–$60,000. **Growth Through 2018:** Probably low. **Annual Job Openings:** No data available.

Career Cluster(s): 04 Business, Management, and Administration; 13 Manufacturing. **Knowledge/Courses:** No data available. **Interests:** Data—High, People—Medium, Things—High.

■ **Industrial Ecologists.** Study or investigate industrial production and natural ecosystems to achieve high production, sustainable resources, and environmental safety or protection. May apply principles and activities of natural ecosystems to develop models for industrial systems.

Green Sector(s): Energy Efficiency. **Role in the Green Economy:** By studying the inputs and outputs of commercial activities and how these relate to the larger environment, industrial ecologists find ways for businesses to operate in a more sustainable manner.

Education/Training Required: Master's degree. **Average Annual Earnings:** No data available. **Growth Through 2018:** No data available. **Annual Job Openings:** No data available.

Career Cluster(s): 01 Agriculture, Food, and Natural Resources. **Knowledge/Courses:** No data available. **Interests:** Data—High, People—Medium, Things—Medium.

■ **Industrial Machinery Mechanics and Millwrights.** Repair, install, adjust, or maintain industrial production and processing machinery or refinery and pipeline distribution systems.

Green Sector(s): Manufacturing. **Role in the Green Economy:** Industrial machinery mechanics and millwrights are finding ways to make machines run with greater energy efficiency. They also install and repair the large and complex machines that generate power from renewable resources. Finally, these workers maintain the machines that manufacture many products related to energy conservation, such as photoelectric cells, fiberglass insulation, and wind turbine blades.

Education/Training Required: Moderate-term on-the-job training; long-term on-the-job training. **Average Annual Earnings:** $43,707. **Growth Through 2018:** Low. **Annual Job Openings:** 8,730.

Career Cluster(s): 13 Manufacturing. **Knowledge/Courses:** Mechanical; Building and Construction; Engineering and Technology; Design; Physics; Chemistry; Mathematics; Public Safety and Security. **Interests:** Data—Medium, People—Low, Things—Very high.

■ **Insulation Workers.** Install the materials used to insulate buildings and equipment.

Green Sector(s): Energy Efficiency; Green Construction. **Role in the Green Economy:** Insulation is vital for conserving energy, so the workers who install it play an important role in reducing America's dependence on nonrenewable resources. New buildings are being constructed with greater use of insulation, and leaky old buildings are being retrofitted with better-quality insulation. Insulation workers are also improving the efficiency of industrial processes by slowing the leakage of heat.

Education/Training Required: Moderate-term on-the-job training. **Average Annual Earnings:** $34,920. **Growth Through 2018:** High. **Annual Job Openings:** 2,870.

Career Cluster(s): 02 Architecture and Construction. **Knowledge/Courses:** Building and Construction; Design; Transportation; Production and Processing; Foreign Language; Food Production; Physics; Engineering and Technology. **Interests:** Data—Low, People—Medium, Things—High.

▨ **Landscape Architects.** Plan and design land areas for such projects as parks and other recreational facilities; airports; highways; hospitals; schools; land subdivisions; and commercial, industrial, and residential sites.

Green Sector(s): Agriculture and Forestry; Environmental Protection; Green Construction; Research, Design, and Consulting Services. **Role in the Green Economy:** Increasingly, landscape architects work in environmental remediation, such as preservation and restoration of wetlands or abatement of stormwater run-off in new developments. Historic landscape preservation and restoration is another area where landscape architects increasingly play a role and where they can conserve energy and materials by finding ways to accommodate historic landscape features to new uses. They also help prepare environmental impact statements for proposed construction projects that will affect the landscape.

Education/Training Required: Bachelor's degree. **Average Annual Earnings:** $60,560. **Growth Through 2018:** High. **Annual Job Openings:** 980.

Career Cluster(s): 02 Architecture and Construction. **Knowledge/Courses:** Design; Geography; Building and Construction; Fine Arts; Biology; Engineering and Technology; History and Archeology; Sales and Marketing. **Interests:** Data—Very high, People—High, Things—Medium.

▨ **Line Installers and Repairers.** Install and maintain the wires and cables that provide customers with electrical power and services for voice, video, and data communications.

Green Sector(s): Energy Efficiency. **Role in the Green Economy:** As new power plants are commissioned, using renewable energy sources, power lines will need to be strung from new locations where wind and sunshine are plentiful. The transition to a "smart grid" will not require new power lines to be strung, but it will provide work for the line installers and repairers who will upgrade the grid with high-tech equipment for communicating and controlling grid performance.

Education/Training Required: Long-term on-the-job training. **Average Annual Earnings:** $52,146. **Growth Through 2018:** Little change. **Annual Job Openings:** 7,340.

Career Cluster(s): 02 Architecture and Construction; 13 Manufacturing. **Knowledge/Courses:** Telecommunications; Building and Construction;

Mechanical; Customer and Personal Service; Engineering and Technology; Transportation; Design; Public Safety and Security. **Interests:** Data—Medium, People—Medium, Things—Very high.

▓ Methane/Landfill Gas Production Workers. Operate, maintain, and manage facilities that collect gas from landfills and process it as a substitute for natural gas.

Green Sector(s): Recycling and Waste Reduction. **Role in the Green Economy:** Landfill gas is not a renewable resource, but it replaces natural gas that would have to be obtained by more environmentally disruptive drilling. Most important of all, the combustion of the gas for commercial purposes transforms the methane to a less threatening greenhouse gas, carbon dioxide, and creates fewer smog-causing air pollutants than would be produced if the unrefined gas were simply flared off at the landfill site. Landfills that have invested in energy-producing equipment tend to be more careful to avoid losing gas to surface leaks. Production of biogas from livestock manure reduces the bacterial content of the waste, controls odors, and creates a solid byproduct that is useful as a fertilizer.

Education/Training Required: Work experience in a related occupation. **Average Annual Earnings:** $40,000–$60,000. **Growth Through 2018:** Probably high. **Annual Job Openings:** No data available.

Career Cluster(s): 04 Business, Management, and Administration; 13 Manufacturing. **Knowledge/Courses:** No data available. **Interests:** Data—High, People—Medium, Things—High.

▓ Physicists. Conduct research to understand the nature of the universe and everything in it.

Green Sector(s): Research, Design, and Consulting Services. **Role in the Green Economy:** Many breakthrough discoveries in the field of renewable energy, such as photovoltaic cells with greater efficiency, depend on the research of physicists and the development work of people trained in physics. Physicists also find ways to monitor the environment. For example, the Antarctic hole in the atmosphere's ozone layer was discovered by three British geophysicists.

Education/Training Required: Doctoral degree. **Average Annual Earnings:** $106,251. **Growth Through 2018:** High. **Annual Job Openings:** 760.

Career Cluster(s): 15 Science, Technology, Engineering, and Mathematics. **Knowledge/Courses:** Physics; Mathematics; Engineering and Technology; Computers and Electronics; Chemistry; English Language; Telecommunications; Communications and Media. **Interests:** Data—High, People—Medium, Things—Low.

■ **Plumbers, Pipelayers, Pipefitters, and Steamfitters.** Install, maintain, and repair many different types of pipe systems.

Green Sector(s): Green Construction. **Role in the Green Economy:** Apart from photovoltaic power, all renewable energy sources involve pipe systems and provide jobs for pipelayers, pipefitters, steamfitters, and in some cases plumbers. Pipe systems are used to carry steam from geothermal heat, ethanol from biofuels distilleries, methane gas from landfills, and warm water from rooftop solar panels. Pipelayers may install a network of pipes that circulate water underground to absorb warmth for a heat pump, or they may lay a pipeline that carries purified landfill gas to homes that burn it.

Education/Training Required: Short-term on-the-job training; long-term on-the-job training. **Average Annual Earnings:** $44,922. **Growth Through 2018:** High. **Annual Job Openings:** 19,830.

Career Cluster(s): 02 Architecture and Construction. **Knowledge/Courses:** Building and Construction; Mechanical; Physics; Design; Engineering and Technology; Transportation; Chemistry; Food Production. **Interests:** Data—Medium, People—Medium, Things—Very high.

■ **Power Plant Operators, Distributors, and Dispatchers.** Control the production and distribution of electric power.

Green Sector(s): Energy and Carbon Capture and Storage; Renewable Energy Generation. **Role in the Green Economy:** As the nation builds more power plants based on renewable energy resources, more power plant operators, distributors, and dispatchers are working with new kinds of equipment and safety systems. As power generated from wind and sunshine becomes more widespread, the intermittent availability of these resources will create new challenges for power distributors and dispatchers, who will also receive new kinds of network feedback when the planned "smart grid" is developed. These workers' jobs are already changing as thousands of rooftops are becoming miniature power plants, pumping power into the grid on sunny days.

Education/Training Required: Long-term on-the-job training. **Average Annual Earnings:** $62,821. **Growth Through 2018:** Little change. **Annual Job Openings:** 1,840.

Career Cluster(s): 13 Manufacturing. **Knowledge/Courses:** Physics; Mechanical; Chemistry; Engineering and Technology; Public Safety and Security; Building and Construction; Design; Telecommunications. **Interests:** Data—Medium, People—Medium, Things—High.

■ **Roofers.** Cover roofs of structures with shingles, slate, asphalt, aluminum, wood, and related materials. May spray roofs, sidings, and walls with material to bind, seal, insulate, or soundproof sections of structures.

Green Sector(s): Green Construction. **Role in the Green Economy:** The roof is where the most sunlight strikes our homes and our less-tall buildings. It is also up beyond most hazards, apart from the occasional pop-up fly ball from a backyard ball game. That means it is usually the perfect place to locate solar panels to generate electricity or heat water. Many roofing contractors offer to install solar panels and train some of their roofers in the skills required for that work. Roofs that are literally green, with grasses or other plantings, absorb less heat than a conventional roof and produce less water runoff during storms.

Education/Training Required: Moderate-term on-the-job training. **Average Annual Earnings:** $33,970. **Growth Through 2018:** Low. **Annual Job Openings:** 3,010.

Career Cluster(s): 02 Architecture and Construction. **Knowledge/Courses:** Building and Construction; Design; Fine Arts; Foreign Language; Engineering and Technology; Transportation; Production and Processing; History and Archeology. **Interests:** Data—Low, People—Medium, Things—High.

■ **Science Technicians.** Assist scientists by using principles and theories of science and mathematics to solve problems in research and development and to help invent and improve products and processes.

Green Sector(s): Agriculture and Forestry; Environmental Protection; Manufacturing; Renewable Energy Generation; Research, Design, and Consulting Services. **Role in the Green Economy:** As the economy shifts to a more sustainable model, a lot of science is being done and thousands of technicians are getting involved. Some are helping to research new forms of energy production, testing for quality control of solar panels, monitoring pollution of the air and water, detecting pests that threaten crops or forests, and locating promising sources of geothermal heat.

Education/Training Required: Associate degree; bachelor's degree. **Average Annual Earnings:** $40,963. **Growth Through 2018:** Average. **Annual Job Openings:** 12,380.

Career Cluster(s): 01 Agriculture, Food, and Natural Resources; 08 Health Science; 12 Law, Public Safety, Corrections, and Security; 13 Manufacturing; 15 Science, Technology, Engineering, and Mathematics. **Knowledge/ Courses:** Chemistry; Biology; Physics; Engineering and Technology; Mechanical; Computers and Electronics; Mathematics; Geography. **Interests:** Data—Medium, People—Low, Things—Medium.

■ **Sheet Metal Workers.** Fabricate, assemble, install, and repair sheet metal products and equipment, such as ducts, control boxes, drainpipes, and furnace casings. Work may involve any of the following: setting up and operating fabricating machines to cut, bend, and straighten sheet metal; shaping metal over anvils, blocks, or forms, using hammer; operating soldering and welding equipment to join sheet metal parts; and inspecting, assembling, and smoothing seams and joints of burred surfaces.

Green Sector(s): Green Construction; Manufacturing; Renewable Energy Generation. **Role in the Green Economy:** One important green role for sheet metal workers is in installing and servicing high-efficiency heating and air-conditioning systems, including those that use solar or geothermal heat. Another is building commissioning, which means a thorough evaluation of the efficiency of a building's HVAC, electrical, lighting, plumbing, fire safety, and security systems. Obviously, a higher level of knowledge and skill is needed to do this work. A third green role is in the manufacture of solar panels and wind turbines.

Education/Training Required: Long-term on-the-job training. **Average Annual Earnings:** $40,640. **Growth Through 2018:** Low. **Annual Job Openings:** 5,170.

Career Cluster(s): 13 Manufacturing. **Knowledge/Courses:** Building and Construction; Design; Mechanical; Engineering and Technology; Production and Processing; Physics; Mathematics; Administration and Management. **Interests:** Data—Low, People—Medium, Things—High.

Solar Energy Production Workers. Operate, maintain, and manage facilities that collect heat or generate electric energy from sunlight.

Green Sector(s): Renewable Energy Generation. **Role in the Green Economy:** You don't have to be a technician or manager to work in the field of solar energy. Many other kinds of workers are needed—such as those in communications, community outreach, sales/marketing, and business support (e.g., finance, accounting, human resources, law, and information technology). To see examples of the variety of jobs in solar energy technologies, look at the current job openings listed at www.ases.org (click "JOBS").

Education/Training Required: Moderate-term on-the-job training; associate degree. **Average Annual Earnings:** $25,000–$50,000. **Growth Through 2018:** Probably very high. **Annual Job Openings:** No data available.

Career Cluster(s): 04 Business, Management, and Administration; 13 Manufacturing. **Knowledge/Courses:** No data available. **Interests:** Data—High, People—Medium, Things—High.

Surveyors, Cartographers, Photogrammetrists, and Surveying and Mapping Technicians. Measure and map the Earth's surface.

Green Sector(s): Green Construction. **Role in the Green Economy:** Planning for a more sustainable economy requires accurate information on locations of renewable energy sources such as hot rock formations or strong winds; of routes taken by commuting drivers who would most benefit from construction of a light rail line; of forest areas most vulnerable to wildfires; of waterways suffering from pollution; or of the contours of a property on which a biofuels plant will be built. Specialists are needed to gather this data, organize it in geographical databases, and represent it in maps.

Education/Training Required: Moderate-term on-the-job training; bachelor's degree. **Average Annual Earnings:** $45,522. **Growth Through 2018:** High. **Annual Job Openings:** 5,910.

Career Cluster(s): 02 Architecture and Construction; 07 Government and Public Administration; 13 Manufacturing; 15 Science, Technology, Engineering, and Mathematics. **Knowledge/Courses:** Geography; Design; Mathematics; Engineering and Technology; Computers and Electronics; Building and Construction; History and Archeology; Law and Government. **Interests:** Data—High, People—Medium, Things—Medium.

■ **Urban and Regional Planners.** Sustainability issues have become important concerns for urban and regional planners. For example, as suburban growth and economic development have created more jobs outside cities, they have also created a need for public transportation to replace gasoline-consuming, fume-emitting cars to get workers to those jobs. In response, planners are developing and modeling possible transportation systems and explaining them to planning boards and the general public. Environmental planners are working to soften the impacts of development, to protect agricultural land and open spaces, and to find ways to rehabilitate polluted former sites of industry.

Green Sector(s): Governmental and Regulatory Administration; Green Construction; Research, Design, and Consulting Services. **Role in the Green Economy:** Sustainability issues have become important concerns for urban and regional planners. For example, as suburban growth and economic development have created more jobs outside cities, they have also created a need for public transportation to replace cars to get workers to those jobs. In response, planners are developing and modeling possible transportation systems and explaining them to planning boards and the general public. Environmental planners are working to minimize the adverse impacts of development, to protect agricultural land and open spaces, and to find ways to rehabilitate polluted former sites of industry.

Education/Training Required: Master's degree. **Average Annual Earnings:** $61,820. **Growth Through 2018:** High. **Annual Job Openings:** 1,470.

Career Cluster(s): 07 Government and Public Administration. **Knowledge/ Courses:** Geography; History and Archeology; Transportation; Design; Law and Government; Building and Construction; Sociology and Anthropology; Economics and Accounting. **Interests:** Data—Medium, People—Medium, Things—Very low.

▨ Water and Liquid Waste Treatment Plant and System Operators.
Operate or control an entire process or system of machines, often through the use of control boards, to transfer or treat water or liquid waste.

Green Sector(s): Environmental Protection. **Role in the Green Economy:** For many decades, wastewater treatment plants have been essential for preserving the health of rivers and groundwater supplies. As interest in a sustainable economy continues to grow, engineers are taking a new look at sewage, which contains 10 times as much energy as is needed to process it, and are finding ways to extract that energy. Some wastewater treatment plants are capturing methane gas from wastewater and using it as a substitute for natural gas. Other plants are processing combustible solids from the wastewater stream to create renewable fuel.

Education/Training Required: Long-term on-the-job training. **Average Annual Earnings:** $39,850. **Growth Through 2018:** High. **Annual Job Openings:** 4,690.

Career Cluster(s): 01 Agriculture, Food, and Natural Resources. **Knowledge/ Courses:** Physics; Building and Construction; Mechanical; Biology; Chemistry; Engineering and Technology; Public Safety and Security; Design. **Interests:** Data—Medium, People—Medium, Things—High.

▨ Water Resource Specialists.
Design or implement programs and strategies related to water resource issues such as supply, quality, and regulatory compliance.

Green Sector(s): Environmental Protection. **Role in the Green Economy:** Clean water is vital to human health and to a healthy environment. Water resource specialists ensure that communities will be able to obtain high-quality water and will not pollute water resources that support other communities and wildlife.

Education/Training Required: Bachelor's or higher degree plus experience. **Average Annual Earnings:** No data available. **Growth Through 2018:** No data available. **Annual Job Openings:** No data available.

Career Cluster(s): 15 Science, Technology, Engineering, and Mathematics. **Knowledge/Courses:** No data available. **Interests:** Data—Medium, People—Medium, Things—Medium.

■ **Weatherization Installers and Technicians.** Perform a variety of activities to weatherize homes and make them more energy efficient. Duties include repairing windows; insulating ducts; and performing heating, ventilating, and air-conditioning (HVAC) work. May perform energy audits and advise clients on energy conservation measures.

Green Sector(s): Energy Efficiency. **Role in the Green Economy:** Weatherization helps society in several ways. By reducing consumption of energy for heating and cooling, it reduces the generation of greenhouse gases from power plants, furnaces, and water heaters. It also saves money for businesses, which makes them more competitive, and for householders. Weatherization also maintains the value of residential and commercial buildings, reducing the amount of demolition and rebuilding that is needed and preserving the architectural character of communities.

Education/Training Required: Short-term on-the-job training; associate degree. **Average Annual Earnings:** $20,000–$40,000. **Growth Through 2018:** Probably high. **Annual Job Openings:** No data available.

Career Cluster(s): 13 Manufacturing. **Knowledge/Courses:** No data available. **Interests:** Data—Medium, People—Low, Things—High.

■ **Welding, Soldering, and Brazing Workers.** Use molten metal to join metal parts or to fill holes, indentations, or seams of metal products.

Green Sector(s): Green Construction; Manufacturing. **Role in the Green Economy:** Welders, brazers, and solderers play important roles in the construction and repair of facilities for production of renewable energy. Welding and brazing workers are needed to assemble the pipes in biofuels production plants and the towers that hold up wind turbines. Welding machine operators may fabricate the frames that hold photovoltaic cells. Even in traditional energy industries, welders can go green by using modern equipment that uses energy more efficiently.

Education/Training Required: Postsecondary vocational training. **Average Annual Earnings:** $34,542. **Growth Through 2018:** Little change. **Annual Job Openings:** 14,290.

Career Cluster(s): 13 Manufacturing. **Knowledge/Courses:** Mechanical; Production and Processing; Engineering and Technology; Building and Construction; Design. **Interests:** Data—Low, People—Low, Things—High.

■ **Wind Energy Production Workers.** Operate, maintain, and manage facilities that generate energy from wind power.

Green Sector(s): Renewable Energy Generation. **Role in the Green Economy:** You don't have to be a technician or manager to work in the field of wind energy production. The industry supports many kinds of jobs—

such as those in communications, community outreach, sales/marketing, and business support (e.g., finance, accounting, human resources, law, and information technology). To see examples of the variety of jobs in wind energy technologies, look at the current job openings listed at www.eco.org or www.careersinwind.com.

Education/Training Required: Work experience in a related occupation; associate degree. **Average Annual Earnings:** $40,000–$50,000. **Growth Through 2018:** Probably very high. **Annual Job Openings:** No data available.

Career Cluster(s): 04 Business, Management, and Administration; 13 Manufacturing. **Knowledge/Courses:** No data available. **Interests:** Data— High, People—Medium, Things—High.

Key Points: Step 5

- The jobs described in this chapter are a highly diverse set.

- Accurate information about specific jobs is a key part of career planning, but the descriptions here cover only the highlights of each job.

- The jobs described in this chapter appear in a longer form in JIST's edition of the *Occupational Outlook Handbook*.

 # STEP 6: Find Green Job Openings

It's never too early to start researching job openings. Even if you're still undecided about your career goal, you should find out about job opportunities in the community where you want to live and work. Why waste your time, money, and energy preparing for a career that has few job openings? If you're going to need to relocate to find work in your chosen field, isn't it better to know that now?

On the other hand, maybe you're much further along in the career-planning process. Maybe you've already made up your mind about your career goal. You may even have completed the expected entry requirements, so you're ready to apply for a job in your targeted occupation. But before you put on your job-interview clothes, you need to learn how to conduct a job search.

Preparing for the Job Hunt

Big-game hunters always bring the right weapons and ammo, and green-job hunters also need to gear up for their efforts. To start, you need to have your resume in good shape so you can send it off on short notice. The resume needs to show a tight focus on the kind of job you want and the strengths you bring to the employer. The cover letter also should be based on this focused thinking.

This book does not have room for examples of resumes and cover letters, but here are some helpful JIST books about these documents:

- *Résumé Magic: Trade Secrets of a Professional Résumé Writer,* by Susan Britton Whitcomb

- *Cover Letter Magic: Trade Secrets of Professional Resume Writers,* by Wendy S. Enelow and Louise M. Kursmark

- *30-Minute Resume Makeover,* by Louise M. Kursmark

- *Amazing Resumes,* by Jim Bright, Ph.D., and Joanne Earl, Ph.D.

Another tool in your job-hunting kit is the "elevator speech," which you should prepare and rehearse before you start pursuing job leads. This is a brief statement of who you are, what kind of job you're seeking, and why you qualify for this kind of job. No matter where you use this speech, it must be concise enough that you could say it to someone on an elevator and get all your points across before the elevator has stopped.

Finding Green Jobs

You may have already heard about the "hidden job market." Studies have revealed that most jobs are found not by answering an advertisement in a newspaper or by waiting for a Web site to match you to an employer, but rather through personal contacts. This is true for all kinds of jobs, but especially for specialized work such as green jobs.

There are two basic strategies for finding out about unadvertised jobs: *cold-calling* employers who hire people for green jobs or *networking* so that you hear about potential green job openings. The two overlap to some extent: Through a cold call to an employer, you may hear about a possible green job elsewhere, and through your network, you may hear about employers who are most likely to be worth cold-calling. You can pursue both strategies simultaneously.

Both networking and cold-calling require you to move outside your comfort zone. Your problem is that you don't know about the hidden green job openings. You won't learn about them by talking only to your friends, because your friends tend to know most of the same things you know. The principle behind networking is that by connecting to the people your friends know you can learn information (in this case, about green jobs) that ordinarily would not be available to you. The principle behind cold-calling is that by talking directly to the people who make hiring decisions, you can learn about green jobs that may never be advertised.

Green Networking

In networking, the usual procedure is to make a list of everyone you know, call them, give them your elevator speech, and make it clear to them what sort of work you're looking for. You may also find it useful to ask them for advice and look on this as a final stage of career exploration. For example, you might ask them what green industries or businesses need people like you, or you might ask whether they know anyone who does this kind of green work and what that person's experiences have been. Conversations like this plant a seed: These people now think of you as a job-seeker in the green career field and may later relay to you news of a job opening. More likely, they will be able to tell you the name of someone who is more knowledgeable about the green industry you have in mind, and *that* person may be your actual lead for a job opening. Make a point of asking for the name of someone who knows lots of people in the green field you're targeting. Studies of networks show that most contacts are made through a small number of very well-connected people.

Because you're looking for work in a specific field—one of the green industries—you need to expand your network in that green industry and not rely only on the random connections of the people you already know.

A good place to start is LinkedIn.com, a Web site designed for networking. If you have not already joined, you may find it a useful way of connecting with friends, former classmates, and former business associates to let them know your career interests. The site offers tools for getting your contacts to write recommendations for you and for helping you get in touch with their contacts. Because you're looking for a green job, you'll be especially interested in a LinkedIn group you can join: the Green Jobs & Career Network. On the group page, you can participate in discussion of green career issues, read news about green industry events and green organizations, and find postings of green job openings.

Don't limit your networking to the Web. Face-to-face networking can be very powerful, so try to find local chapters of groups that meet to promote green causes, such as the Sierra Club, the National Audubon Society, the Arbor Day Foundation, the Izaak Walton League of America, or the Nature Conservancy. Some local organizations that don't have a national profile may be active in your community; search for them at www.meetup.org. Many of these organizations are looking for volunteers or holding regular meetings.

For an atmosphere that is more social and less cause-oriented, you might attend a local meeting of Green Drinks. This networking group tends to meet in restaurants, bars, or bookstores.

Cold-Calling Green Employers

Someone in your network may mention your name to a manager who is hiring for a green job, and that person may give you a call. But, in many situations, the person in your network will give you the name of someone who is hiring, and it will be up to you to make the call. In that case, you are shifting to the cold-calling strategy.

You don't have to wait for your network to turn up likely employers to call. The most effective way to conduct a cold-calling campaign is to research the businesses that hire people for the kind of green job you seek. Business directories such as the Yellow Pages can help, but for green occupations, a more productive source for learning about employing businesses is a professional association.

Some notable green-industry groups are the Solar Energy Industries Association, the American Wind Energy Association, and the U.S. Green Building Council. But remember that most employers of green workers belong to traditional industry groups, such as the American Society of Heating, Refrigerating, and Air-Conditioning Engineers; the National Electrical Contractors Association; or the American Welding Society. If the association has a membership directory, note which companies employ a lot of members. Another clue is to observe which businesses sponsor the association or its activities.

You should also consider small employers. The Green VC blog (www.greenvc.org) is a Web site where you can identify start-up companies in green industries.

When you have identified a likely business, don't contact the human resources department; they know only about the part of the job market that isn't hidden. Instead, find the name and phone number of someone who has the power to make a hiring decision. In a small company, this may be the CEO or other top manager; in a large company, it may be a department head. Telephone this person. If you call between 8 and 9 in the morning or 5 and 6 in the evening, you may improve the odds that the phone will be answered by the person you seek rather than by a secretary. If you get the person's voice mailbox, hang up and try again at another time; cold calls are unlikely to be returned. E-mail takes less courage than the telephone, but it is too easily lost in the pile of messages cluttering your target's inbox and may automatically be flagged as spam.

When you are talking to a person who can make a hiring decision, you have two tactics open to you: direct and indirect. The direct method is to give your elevator speech, make it clear that you are interested in a job, and ask for an interview. Be prepared to ask several times, because this shows your interest and determination. Don't ask whether the business has job openings, but perhaps ask if the business is likely to have openings in the future. If the person on the other end says that the company is not hiring now, ask for a get-acquainted interview—maybe a lunch date. At the very least, ask for leads to people who might be hiring for green jobs elsewhere, call those leads, and tell them who referred you. Expect a lot of rejection, but keep in mind that these calls take only a few minutes, so you can cover a large number of employers in one afternoon.

The indirect method is similar—it uses an elevator speech about your background and aims for an interview—but it stops short of asking for a job interview. Instead, you treat the person like a highly targeted networking contact; the goal is an interview that will focus on learning more information rather than on being hired. For example, you might say that you are thinking of specializing in the kind of green work that goes on in that person's business and you want to learn more about the pros and cons of that specialization. If the person on the other end tries to cut you off by saying that the company is not hiring, make it clear that you are not asking for a job interview–you want information or perhaps advice. The informational interview may not, in fact, lead to a job at that company—at least not at present—but it may lead to a future job offer, and at least it has a good chance of taking your networking campaign to a higher level. This person is much more likely than your second cousin or your high school friend to know someone in another department or a similar business who has a green job opening.

Job Postings

Although most job openings are not posted and advertised jobs attract a lot of competing job candidates, you may want to spend some of your job-hunting time looking at postings. These Web sites specialize in green job postings:

- Green Collar Blog (www.greencollarblog.org)
- Green Jobs Network (www.greenjobs.net)
- Greenjobs (www.greenjobs.com)
- Sustainable Business.com (www.sustainablebusiness.com)
- Green Energy Jobs Network (www.greenenergyjobsnetwork.com)

Because many green jobs are in nonprofit organizations, you may want to look at job boards that specialize in these employers:

- Idealist.org (www.idealist.org)
- Non Profit Jobs (www.nonprofit-jobs.org)
- Jobs for Change (jobs.change.org)

Note that these job postings can also be useful leads for cold calls. The jobs that an employer advertises may be too high-level for you (Executive Director), too low-level for you (unpaid intern), or just not in your area of specialization, but the same employer may be hiring for additional jobs that are not posted (or not posted yet).

Job Hunting Is a Job

Accept the idea that job hunting is a job in itself. Make a schedule of your job-hunting activities and stick to it. It helps to schedule differing activities in the same day, partly because some activities work best at specific times of day and partly because you can get bored and discouraged if you spend the whole day doing only one kind of job-hunting task.

Key Points: Step 6

- It's important to know about job openings even before you've made up your mind about your career goal.

- Before you start your job hunt, you need to write a well-focused resume and cover letter. You also need to develop and practice an "elevator speech."

- Networking and cold-calling allow you to tap into the hidden job market, where most jobs are filled. Specialized networks have been developed for the green industries.

- Specialized job boards can help you identify green job openings or employers who may have other unadvertised green jobs.